IRAN

VIOLATIONS OF HUMAN RIGHTS
1987 - 1990

AI Index: MDE 13/21/90
ISBN: 0 86210 188 3
First Published December 1990
Amnesty International Publications
1 Easton Street
London WC1X 8DJ
United Kingdom

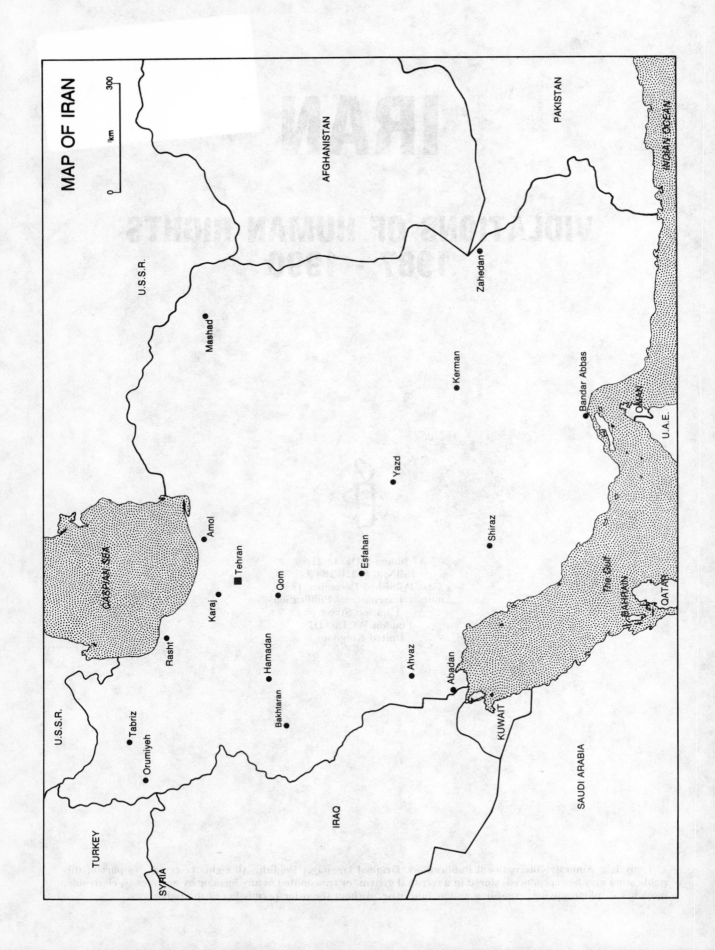

MAP OF IRAN

300

1km

0

U.S.S.R.

TURKEY

SYRIA

IRAQ

U.S.S.R.

Orumiyeh

Tabriz

Rasht

CASPIAN SEA

Amol

Tehran

Karaj

Hamadan

Bakhtaran

Qom

Esfahan

Mashad

Yazd

Kerman

Shiraz

Ahvaz

Abadan

KUWAIT

SAUDI ARABIA

The Gulf

BAHRAIN

QATAR

Bandar Abbas

OMAN

U.A.E.

Zahedan

AFGHANISTAN

PAKISTAN

INDIAN OCEAN

IRAN: VIOLATIONS OF HUMAN RIGHTS 1987-1990

LIST OF CONTENTS

INTRODUCTION

Amnesty International has been concerned for many years about serious
human rights violations in Iran, both during the reign of the Shah and
after the Islamic Revolution of 1979.

The organization published its last major report on Iran, <u>Iran: Violations
of Human Rights</u> (AI Index MDE 13/09/87) in 1987. Three years later the
violations of human rights described in that report continue, and include
the execution of thousands of people after unfair trials.

This report does not claim to be an up-to-date record of all human
rights violations committed in Iran -- such an aim would be unrealistic
given the constraints on information gathering in Iran faced by independent
human rights monitors. Instead, it identifies and presents patterns of
human rights violations that have occurred between January 1987 and July
1990.

Arbitrary arrest and unfair trial of political prisoners, including
prisoners of conscience, continue in Iran. Torture and the application of
punishments which constitute cruel, inhuman or degrading treatment remain
widespread. Thousands of people were executed between 1987 and 1990
including more than 2,000 political prisoners between July 1988 and January
1989. This report records the activities of a group of government
officials known to prisoners as the "Death Commission": the group reviewed
the cases of political prisoners in Tehran's Evin Prison and Gohardasht
Prison in Karaj, sending hundreds of them to their deaths in the latter
part of 1988. Many of those who died had been imprisoned for their non-
violent political activity.

Amnesty International's 1987 report contained comprehensive
recommendations designed to bring legislation and practice in Iran into
conformity with international human rights standards. Amnesty International
has not received a substantive reply from the Iranian authorities to the
issues raised in its 1987 report. As little, if any, progress appears to
have been made towards the implementation of these recommendations, many of
which are repeated in this report, the case for their implementation has
been strengthened by the sad record of a further three years of human
rights abuse.

Amnesty International has repeatedly sought to discuss its concerns
with responsible ministers and other officials in Iran. Since 1987 no
official reply to these requests has been received and the organization has
been obliged to carry out its research from outside the country.
Independent domestic human rights organizations are unable to operate
within the country, and there is no independent Bar Association. Lawyers
were among the first to be imprisoned as prisoners of conscience and forced
into exile as political repression grew in 1980 and 1981. These practical
difficulties impede the flow of information about human rights abuses in
Iran to the rest of the world, and present problems in verifying reports of

violations. In addition, witnesses to human rights abuse are often reluctant to come forward due to fear of reprisals by the authorities against their relatives living in Iran or their loved ones in prison.

In spite of these problems, information about human rights abuses in Iran does emerge. Former prisoners and other witnesses to human rights violations have taken great risks to leave the country. They join the hundreds of thousands of Iranians driven into exile by decades of political repression in Iran. Some of these witnesses have told their stories to Amnesty International. Relatives of political prisoners have pieced together information transmitted through letters and telephone calls from inside Iran despite the risk of interception by the authorities. It has often taken months or even years for a full picture of events to take shape. In mid-1990 Amnesty International was still receiving new information about the massacre of political prisoners which had begun two years earlier.

There are other sources of information available to Amnesty International. Within the confined territory available for political discussion in Iran, which is almost entirely restricted to the country's clerical leadership, there is a lively press. Human rights issues are often discussed in Iranian newspapers, and personalities representing conflicting currents within the leadership have expressed strong views in Parliament and elsewhere on matters relating to human rights. Amnesty International's 1987 report on Iran was the subject of comment on the floor of Parliament.

Opposition groups in exile have also publicized alleged human rights violations in Iran. Many of these allegations are impossible to verify and some are exaggerated for political motives. Nevertheless, information from a wide variety of opposition groups has, when matched with other sources of information, provided persuasive evidence of a continuing pattern of widespread human rights abuse in Iran.

The Political Context

The war with Iraq was a dominant political factor in Iran throughout the 1980s. Fighting began in September 1980 when the Iraqi Government, apparently seeking to take advantage of perceived disarray in the Iranian armed forces following the February 1979 revolution, tried to reassert Iraqi claims over disputed border territories, including three islands in the Straits of Hormuz.

By 1987 both sides had suffered heavy casualties. A major Iranian offensive on the Iraqi city of Basra had been held up by the Iraqi forces, and repeated attempts by Iranian troops to achieve a decisive breakthrough by use of "human wave" tactics had been repulsed. Iranian cities had come under long-range aerial bombardment during the "war of the cities". Attacks on merchant shipping by both sides had increased the presence of US naval forces in the Gulf region.

As a result, diplomatic attempts to end the fighting gained momentum. On 20 July 1987 the United Nations (UN) Security Council adopted Resolution 598 which called for a ceasefire, a withdrawal to internationally recognized borders, and the beginning of peace negotiations. Iranian leaders resisted pressure to accept the resolution, but shortages of arms, ammunition and spare parts for weapons, made it increasingly difficult for Iran to continue to fight the war. Domestic pressure from a war-weary population, and influential opinion within the leadership that there was little to be gained from a continuation of the fighting, led to the announcement on 18 July 1988 that Iran was ready to accept the ceasefire. In a telling statement indicating the Iranian leadership's commitment to the war effort, Ayatollah Khomeini said that "taking this decision was more deadly for me than taking poison". The ceasefire came into effect in August 1988 but by July 1990 no peace treaty had been signed, and the vast majority of prisoners of war remained in detention.

The state of war had a pervasive influence on Iranian society in the 1980s. The decade was marked by a lack of progress towards the establishment of institutions and procedures which could have provided Iranian citizens with safeguards of their fundamental human rights. To some extent the Iranian Government was able to mobilize popular support for the war effort against a traditional enemy widely viewed in Iran as the aggressor. The contribution made by the "martyrs", tens of thousands of whom gave their lives for the war effort, was the focal point in the government's rhetoric. Any criticism of government policy, even in fields not directly related to the war, could be portrayed as betrayal of the "martyrs". This contributed to a climate in which dissent from government policy was rarely tolerated.

The war also prolonged the fervour of the post-revolutionary period so that in mid-1990, over 11 years after the overthrow of the Shah, the Iranian leadership was still debating fundamental questions about the structure of the judiciary and the executive in the government of the Islamic Republic. Amnesty International's 1987 report noted that Iran's parliament, the Islamic Consultative Assembly (Majles-e Shouray-e Eslami) had approved the Islamic Penal Code for a five-year trial period in 1981. In 1990 Parliament was still discussing the form which Iran's penal code would take. In July 1989 root and branch reform of the judiciary was set in motion by the abolition of the Supreme Judicial Council, the dismissal of its former president, Ayatollah Ardebili, and the appointment of Ayatollah Mohammad Yazdi to the new post of Head of the Judiciary.

The death of Ayatollah Khomeini on 3 June 1989 inevitably meant a change in the style of leadership in Iran. Ayatollah Khomeini had exercised a unique authority, combining an influential political role as the figurehead of the revolution with the status of a senior Shi'a Muslim religious leader. His constitutional role as Leader of the Islamic Republic vested him with absolute powers, but he exercised these in a manner which maintained support for him from all factions within the clerical leadership.

No one person could take the place of Ayatollah Khomeini. His titular role as Leader of the Islamic Republic was taken over by Ayatollah Khamenei, the former president, but effective political power has been exercised by Hojatoleslam Ali Akbar Hashemi Rafsanjani, who was elected President in July 1989.

The imperative to maintain a militant stance is a factor in the continuing widespread abuse of human rights in Iran. Public executions, floggings and amputations are a relatively easy way for the government to demonstrate its uncompromising commitment to revolutionary Islamic values. Curtailing the use of such punishments could be interpreted as capitulation to pressure from the West, and could be exploited by the radical faction to advance its political cause at the expense of the moderates.

Domestic pressure to resist international demands for reform in the human rights field has bestowed a negative connotation on universal human rights standards within some government circles in Iran. This has led some Iranian leaders to assert that Iran is not bound by these international standards.

The record of human rights abuse in Iran has not gone unnoticed by the international community. Since 1984 a Special Representative of the UN Human Rights Commission has examined the human rights situation in Iran with his mandate being renewed annually by the Commission. In 1990, for the first time, the Iranian authorities granted the Special Representative access to Iran. The Special Representative's subsequent report in February 1990 stressed the importance of the Iranian Government providing detailed responses to inquiries about specific incidents of human rights abuse in order to substantiate the government's assertions that it respects human rights.

Political opposition within Iran has been brutally suppressed since the early 1980s. Left-wing groups, monarchists and the largest opposition group, the People's Mojahedine Organization of Iran (PMOI), all spent most of the 1980s operating in exile. The lack of freedom of political expression in Iran makes it difficult to assess the level of support for any of these groups. Repression, which has included the imprisonment and execution of thousands of alleged government opponents, appears to have destroyed the opposition's political structures within the country. The PMOI maintains several thousand troops in Iraq. This force, known as the National Liberation Army, made an incursion into western Iran in July 1988, just prior to the signing of the ceasefire in the Gulf War. Its potential to undertake further substantial attacks would seem to depend on continuing support from the Iraqi Government.

Another factor which continues to influence the human rights situation in Iran is the struggle by ethnic minorities to achieve greater autonomy. Fighting between government forces and Kurdish groups has been in progress in Iranian Kurdistan since the early days of the revolution. During the war with Iraq the principal Kurdish opposition group in Iran, the Kurdish

Democratic Party of Iran (KDPI), received support from Iraq -- just as the Iranian Government offered support to Iraqi Kurds in rebellion against their government. As the war drew to a close the leadership of the KDPI appeared willing to negotiate a truce with the Iranian Government. However, the assassination of Dr Abdul Rahman Ghassemlou, the leader of the KDPI, on 13 July 1989, which evidence suggests was carried out by agents of the Iranian Government, was followed by a resurgence in the fighting in Kurdistan. The KDPI, and the Marxist <u>Komala</u> movement, have suffered the same fate as other political opposition movements in Iran. Hundreds of their members, supporters and sympathizers have been imprisoned and many executed in secret after unfair trials.

Iranian politics now stand at a crossroads. Among the basic demands of the Iranian people which must be met by the government is the respect of their human rights. This report proposes an agenda for immediate action to bring about improvements in the human rights situation in Iran.

CHAPTER ONE: <u>THE DEATH PENALTY</u>

Thousands of prisoners have been executed in Iran since 1987, continuing a trend of extensive use of the death penalty that has characterized the Islamic Republic of Iran since shortly after its foundation in 1979. Dozens of executions for criminal offences, many of them for drug-trafficking, take place every month. In the first six months of 1990 about 300 executions for criminal offences were announced in the official Iranian media. The majority of these were carried out by hanging, often in public. In a few cases execution victims were stoned to death, beheaded, or subjected to a combination of punishments, including flogging and amputation, before being put to death. In 1989 Amnesty International recorded over 1,500 executions announced for criminal offences, more than 1,000 of them for drug-trafficking offences.

<u>Officially announced executions in Iran between 1987 and 1990 recorded by Amnesty International from the Iranian press</u>

<u>1987</u>	<u>1988</u>	<u>1989</u>	<u>1990</u> (January to June only)
158	142	1500	300

(All totals should be regarded as minimum figures.)

Executions of convicted criminals have been running at an exceptionally high level since January 1989 when new anti-drug-trafficking legislation was introduced and when Ayatollah Khomeini instructed the judiciary to speed up the punishment of criminals. The increased use of the death penalty in criminal cases has not been restricted solely to drug-trafficking offences. Executions of people convicted of murder, armed robbery and a variety of other offences have also increased since the beginning of 1989. Amnesty International recorded 158 executions for criminal offences in 1987 and 142 in 1988. More executions were announced during the first six months of 1990 than in 1987 and 1988 together.

Another major aspect of the death penalty in Iran is its extensive use against political opponents. In contrast with criminal executions, which often take place in public and are usually announced in the official media, political executions are usually carried out in secret. For this reason the numbers of political executions which have taken place in Iran are disputed. Amnesty International has recorded the names of over 2,000 prisoners reported to have been the victims of a wave of secret political executions between July 1988 and January 1989. Amnesty International has no way of knowing the full extent of the massacre of political prisoners which took place during this six-month period. However, the organization has interviewed dozens of Iranians whose imprisoned relatives were killed at that time and has received written information about hundreds of other prisoners who were among the victims.

Amnesty International has also spoken to eye-witnesses who were political prisoners in Iran while the mass killings were being carried out. Evidence has also emerged from Iranian Government circles. In particular, letters written in July 1988 to Ayatollah Khomeini by Ayatollah Hossein Ali Montazeri, then the designated successor as Leader of the Islamic Republic, refer to "thousands of executions in a few days" (Reuters, 29 March 1989). Ayatollah Montazeri is also reported to have said: "Many are the innocents and minor offenders who were executed following your last order" (Reuters, 29 March 1989). Taken together, Amnesty International believes that there is overwhelming evidence that in the latter part of 1988 the Iranian Government carried out the largest wave of political executions in Iran since the early 1980s. Reports of political executions continued to reach the organization in 1990, but on a much smaller scale.

1.1   The Death Penalty for Criminal Offences

1.1.1   Scope of Application

The Law of Hodoud (crimes against divine will, singular hadd) and Qisas (retribution) forms part of the Islamic Penal Code of Iran, provisionally approved in 1982 by Iran's Parliament, the Majles-e Shuray-e Eslami (the Islamic Consultative Assembly). It provides for the death penalty for a large number of offences including premeditated murder, rape, and "moral" offences such as adultery, sodomy and repeated counts of drinking alcohol. The Law of Hodoud and Qisas also provides for the death penalty as a possible punishment for those convicted of being mofsed fil arz (corrupt on earth) or mohareb (at enmity with God). Such broad terms can be applied to political opponents, including those expressing their views in a non-violent manner. Speaking at a conference on judicial issues in May 1990, the Head of the Judiciary, Ayatollah Yazdi, made it clear that members of opposition groups such as the PMOI were collectively guilty of "waging war against God" and "corruption on earth" and therefore liable to the death penalty (Ettela'at, 30 May 1990).

The death penalty is an optional punishment for murder, which accounts for approximately 40 per cent of the criminal executions recorded by Amnesty International since 1987. Its enforcement is determined by the Qisas system. This derives from an interpretation of Islamic law and gives the right of retribution to the male next of kin of the murder victim. The next of kin may choose to accept payment (diya), or pardon the murderer instead of exacting the death sentence.

Crimes regarded as Hodoud offences carry a mandatory death sentence. They are regarded as crimes against God and therefore liable to divine retribution. These offences -- such as adultery, sodomy and rape -- account for a much smaller proportion of the criminal executions carried out.

Executions for drug-trafficking offences have increased greatly since January 1989. The death penalty has for many years been part of the Iranian

Government's anti-narcotics policy, both under the Shah and in the Islamic Republic. Government campaigns to combat the activities of drug-traffickers have often been accompanied by an increase in the number of executions of convicted offenders. Mass executions for drug-trafficking in 1989 began even before a new law on drug-trafficking came into force on 21 January, with 56 offenders hanged in towns across Iran on 16 January. The new law provided for a mandatory death sentence for anyone found in possession of more than five kilograms of hashish or opium, or more than 30 grams of heroin, codeine, methadone or morphine.

Between January 1989 and July 1990 over 1,100 people were executed for drug-trafficking, in some cases combined with other charges. Many executions were carried out in public with victims being hanged from cranes in public squares or from a gibbet mounted on the back of a lorry which could then be driven through the streets with the bodies still dangling. On some occasions, large numbers of convicted traffickers were executed on the same day in different towns. On one day in 1989, 81 people were executed. The policy is continuing. On 11 March 1990 the authorities hanged 38 convicted drug-traffickers in 12 cities.

The death penalty is an attractive policy for governments faced with seemingly intractable criminal problems like drug-trafficking. It enables governments to be seen to be taking action which they claim will lead to a solution. For example, on 5 April 1989 the then Prosecutor General, Mohammad Khoeniha, was reported to have made the following reference to the new law on drug-trafficking on Tehran Radio:

> "The implementation of this law has been very successful up to now... We hope that we shall solve this social problem through the decisiveness of the security forces and that the executions will continue until the last smuggler in the country is eliminated." (BBC Summary of World Broadcasts, 6 April 1989)

The persistence of drug-trafficking and drug abuse as social problems in countries like Iran which have employed the death penalty as a major part of anti-narcotics policies is one factor which convinces Amnesty International that the death penalty does not act as a unique deterrent to drug-traffickers. This lack of deterrent effect was cited at the December 1985 meeting of the UN Expert Group on Countermeasures to Drug Smuggling by Air and Sea:

> "... in the experience of several experts, the fact that capital punishment appeared on the statute books as the maximum penalty did not necessarily deter trafficking; indeed in some cases it might make prosecution more difficult because courts of law were naturally inclined to require a much higher standard of proof when capital punishment was possible or even mandatory... The most effective deterrent was assuredly the certainty of detection and arrest." (UN document E/CN.7/1986/11/Add.3)

As already mentioned, the increase in the number of executions for drug-trafficking offences has been accompanied by an increase in the number of executions for other criminal offences. In addition, the scope of application of the death penalty in Iran, already very broad, is being extended to new offences.

For example, the Head of the Judiciary, Ayatollah Mohammad Yazdi, was reported to have made the following remark when speaking about punishments for profiteering on Tehran Radio on 16 March 1990: "[I]f the parliament approves, the judiciary will go as far as execution in dealing with economic terrorists." (Reuters, 16 March 1990.) On 18 July, Parliament ratified a bill which set out punishments, including the death penalty, for such economic offences.

In arguing the case for applying the death penalty to offences associated with profiteering, black-market trading and fraud, direct reference was also made to earlier government campaigns which involved large-scale use of the death penalty. Hojatoleslam Mehdi Karrubi, Speaker of the Islamic Consultative Assembly, is reported to have said in a speech to the Assembly on 18 April 1990:

> "We have crushed the monafeqin [hypocrites, a term used to refer to the PMOI] the leftist groups and the smugglers... This problem will have to be solved. In the same way as the problems of the hypocrites and the smugglers were surgically removed, so will the problem of hoarding, economic terrorism and the like have to be. ...We have already sent so many people to the gallows because they were apostates and enemies of God, and we did it rightly. Now let us send two lots of capitalists to the gallows." (BBC Summary of World Broadcasts, 20 April 1990)

This speech represents perhaps an extreme expression of a government policy which is apparently intoxicated with the death penalty as a catch-all solution to social ills ranging from embezzlement to mass murder. As Speaker Karrubi remarked in the above speech: "It does not matter whether it [execution] solves the problem or not". In some quarters in Iran the death penalty seems to have acquired the status of a virtue in itself, regardless of whether or not the punishment has any discernible effect on the problems it is intended to alleviate.

Amnesty International is opposed to the death penalty in all circumstances and is committed to its abolition in all countries. However, the organization noted in its 1987 report Iran: Violations of Human Rights that:

> "...several of the death penalty provisions in the Law of Hodoud and Qisas do not conform with particular international human rights standards. Article 6(2) of the International Covenant on Civil and Political Rights states: 'In countries which have not abolished the death penalty, sentence of death may be imposed only for the most serious crimes in accordance with the law in force at the time of the commission of the crime...' Many of

the offences for which the Law of <u>Hodoud</u> and <u>Qisas</u> prescribes the death penalty do not involve murder or serious bodily harm constituting the 'most serious crimes', hence imposing the death penalty for these less serious crimes would be incompatible with the terms of Article 6 of the Covenant."

No changes have taken place to detract from the relevance of this observation to the current situation.

1.1.2 <u>Methods of Execution</u>

The overwhelming majority of executions in criminal cases are carried out by hanging, often in public. This may take place on a purpose-built gallows where the prisoner drops to his or her death causing the neck to break. Alternatively, the prisoner may be hauled up by the neck by a crane or pulley, leading to a slower death by strangulation. In many cases whole groups of prisoners have been hauled up in a row to be slowly strangled to death in this way.

There are a number of less frequently used execution methods, including stoning to death, beheading and being forced to jump from a high place. Stoning to death, which is prescribed by the Islamic Penal Code for <u>Hodoud</u> offences such as adultery, prostitution or pimping, has been used to execute dozens of men and women since 1987. Stonings take place in public and spectators are encouraged to participate. According to law, a male prisoner should be buried in a pit up to his waist, while a female is buried up to her chest. The Penal Code is very specific about the types of stones which should be used. Article 119 states, with reference to the penalty for adultery:

> "In the punishment of stoning to death, the stones should not be too large so that the person dies on being hit by one or two of them; they should not be so small either that they could not be defined as stones."

It is clear that the punishment of stoning is designed to cause the victim grievous pain before leading to death.

In early 1990 Amnesty International recorded the first executions carried out by beheading in modern times in Iran. The offence in some of the cases appeared to be male rape.

In February 1990 two men were knifed, then flogged and finally beheaded as a retributive punishment for multiple murder and bank robbery in Hamadan. A third prisoner in this case was flogged and then hanged. The bodies of the three men were displayed around the town and then burned by a mob.

Flogging prior to execution is relatively common. There appears to be a good deal of latitude for the sentencing judge, or for the male next of kin of a murder victim, to choose punishments which they deem appropriate.

Public executions, or processes of execution designed to maximize the suffering of the execution victim, are presumably intended to enhance the deterrent and retributive effects of the death penalty.

Amnesty International believes that the death penalty is the most extreme form of torture and cruel, inhuman and degrading punishment, and a violation of the right to life proclaimed in the Universal Declaration of Human Rights and the International Covenant on Civil and Political Rights (ICCPR). Execution methods specifically designed to increase the suffering of execution victims serve only to heighten Amnesty International's concern in this regard. Flogging, knifing or other forms of corporal punishment prior to execution, including being struck by stones which do not immediately result in death, clearly constitute torture and as such are expressly prohibited by the ICCPR.

1.2 Political Executions

Thousands of political opponents of the government were executed in the early years after the Iranian revolution of 1979. By the mid-1980s, however, reports of political prisoners being executed were much less numerous. However, almost all political executions take place in secret, so it is impossible to be precise about how many were in fact carried out.

Occasionally, the official media indicate that political executions have taken place. For example, in October 1987 the Supreme Judicial Council, at that time responsible for approving death sentences passed by Islamic Revolutionary Courts, was reported to have approved death sentences imposed on "members of atheistic and hypocritical mini-groups" (Keyhan newspaper, 29 October 1987) by courts in west Azerbaijan, Isfahan and Ilam.

Amnesty International has received reports of scores of secret political executions at Evin Prison in Tehran, and in prisons in different parts of the country. The victims are said to have included a group of 40 political prisoners executed in early 1987 for taking part in a hunger-strike to protest about conditions in Evin Prison. In June 1987 Amnesty International learned of the execution of Massoud Ansary, a member of the People's Fedaiyan Organization of Iran (PFOI), who had been held in Evin Prison for two and a half years prior to his execution. In May 1988 the execution in Evin Prison of Anoushirvan Lotfi, Hojatollah Ma'boudi and Hojat Mohammad-Pour, members of different political opposition organizations, was announced in the Iranian press. The report said that these three men were members of the PFOI (Majority), the PMOI and the Union of Communists, and that they had been involved in armed opposition to the government. However, no information was made available about the nature of the evidence against them, nor about the procedures followed at their trials.

Four followers of the Bahai faith, a minority religion in Iran which is not recognized by the Constitution of the Islamic Republic and whose followers have been persecuted since 1979, were reported to have been executed during 1987, apparently because of their religious beliefs.

Approximately 200 Bahais were executed during the early 1980s, but reports of further executions of Bahais have not been received since 1988.

1.2.1 The Massacre of 1988

In mid-1988 the pattern of political executions changed dramatically from piecemeal reports of executions to a massive wave of killings which took place over several months. Even now, two years after these events, it is still not clear how many people died during the six-month period from July 1988 to January 1989. Amnesty International has recorded the names of over 2,000 political prisoners reportedly executed during this period. Iranian opposition groups, such as the PMOI, have suggested that the total was much higher. Speaking on French television in February 1989, Hojatoleslam Rafsanjani is reported to have said that "the number of political prisoners executed in the past few months was less than 1,000" (Iran Yearbook 89/90).

Since these events took place, Amnesty International has interviewed dozens of relatives of execution victims, and a number of former political prisoners who were in prison at the time when the mass killlngs were taking place. It has received written information from many Iranians who believe that their friends or relatives were among the victims. These accounts, taken together with statements by Iranian Government personalities, have convinced Amnesty International that during this six-month period the biggest wave of political executions since the early 1980s took place in Iranian prisons.

Two important political events preceded the executions. On 18 July 1988 Ayatollah Khomeini announced his intention to accept UN Security Council Resolution 598 instituting a ceasefire in the Gulf War between Iran and Iraq. A few days later, the National Liberation Army, a military force formed by the Iraq-based opposition group, the PMOI, staged an armed incursion into western Iran which was repulsed by the Iranian army.

It has been suggested to Amnesty International by former prisoners that both these events may have influenced the government's decision to carry out these executions at this time. The ceasefire in the Gulf War meant that international attention was focused on international developments and not on the situation of political prisoners in Iran. The armed incursion by a PMOI force at a time when the Iranian Government had signalled its intention to cease fighting in the Gulf War gave the authorities a motive to take reprisals against prisoners associated with the PMOI who had been held in prisons around the country, often for several years. Former prisoners have also said that political prisoners were warned by their captors that when the war was over they would be "dealt with".

President Khamenei spoke in December 1988 of the decision taken by the Iranian authorities to execute "those who have links from inside prison with the hypocrites [PMOI] who mounted an armed attack inside the territory of the Islamic Republic". An open letter to Amnesty International from the Permanent Mission of the Islamic Republic of Iran to the UN in New York stated:

"Indeed, authorities of the Islamic Republic of Iran have always denied the existence of any political executions, but that does not contradict other subsequent statements which have confirmed that spies and terrorists have been executed." (UN document A/44/153, 28 February 1989)

The political executions took place in many prisons in all parts of Iran, often far from where the armed incursion took place. Most of the executions were of political prisoners, including an unknown number of prisoners of conscience, who had already served a number of years in prison. They could have played no part in the armed incursion, and they were in no position to take part in spying or terrorist activities. Many of the dead had been tried and sentenced to prison terms during the early 1980s, many for non-violent offences such as distributing newspapers and leaflets, taking part in demonstrations or collecting funds for prisoners' families. Many of the dead had been students in their teens or early twenties at the time of their arrest. The majority of those killed were supporters of the PMOI, but hundreds of members and supporters of other political groups, including various factions of the PFOI, the Tudeh Party, the KDPI, Rah-e Kargar and others, were also among the execution victims.

The first sign that something was happening in the prisons came in July 1988 when family visits to political prisoners were suspended. This was the beginning of months of uncertainty and anguish for prisoners' relatives as rumours began to spread that mass executions of political prisoners were taking place.

No news of the political prisoners was heard for about three months. Relatives would go to prisons on regular visiting days only to be turned away by prison guards. Some brought clothing, medicines or money to the prisons hoping to get a signed receipt from their imprisoned relatives as an indication that they were still alive.

Reports circulated among prisoners' relatives that execution victims were being buried in mass graves. Distraught family members searched the cemeteries for signs of newly dug graves which might contain their relatives' bodies.

One woman described to Amnesty International how she had dug up the corpse of an executed man with her bare hands as she searched for her husband's body in Jadeh Khavaran cemetery in Tehran in August 1988 in a part of the cemetery known colloquially as <u>Lanatabad</u>, (the place of the damned), reserved for the bodies of executed political prisoners.

"Groups of bodies, some clothed, some in shrouds, had been buried in unmarked shallow graves in the section of the cemetery reserved for executed leftist political prisoners. The stench of the corpses was appalling but I started digging with my hands because it was important for me and my two little children that I locate my husband's grave."

She unearthed a body with its face covered in blood but when she cleaned it off she saw that it was not her husband. Other relatives visiting the graveyard discovered her husband's grave some days later. A member of a communist group, he had been arrested in early 1985, tortured over several months and convicted after a summary trial at which, as a result of his torture, he was barely conscious. He never learned what his sentence was. His wife had been turned away from Evin Prison on a regular visiting day in early August, and had then started her quest for information which led her to the unmarked grave.

In October and November 1988 the authorities began to inform families of the execution of their relatives.   In a few cases prison officials informed relatives of the execution when they went to the prison for a normal family visit. This led to protests by prisoners' relatives who gathered outside prisons, so other methods were devised. The majority of relatives appear to have been informed by telephone that they should go to an Islamic Revolutionary Committee office to receive news about their imprisoned relatives. There they were informed of the execution and required to sign undertakings that they would not hold a funeral or any other mourning ceremony. Family members were not informed where their relatives were buried, and even if they managed to find out they were not permitted to erect a gravestone.

An Iranian who left Iran in late 1988 told Amnesty International how his family had learned of the execution of his brother, Hossein. In November 1988 the family received a telephone call instructing the father to go to Evin Prison to receive information about Hossein. Hossein's father and wife went to the prison where they were told that Hossein had been executed because he was not repentant and had not been improved by his imprisonment. They were not informed where his body was, and were told that they should not hold any funeral ceremony.

Hossein had been held in Gohardasht Prison in Karaj where he was serving a 15-year sentence for activities in support of the PMOI. Hossein had been arrested in 1981. His brother told Amnesty International that at that time Hossein had been involved in political activities for the PMOI: collecting money and distributing leaflets and newspapers. His brother is convinced that Hossein was not involved in violent activities.

The mother of a 39-year-old woman executed in Evin Prison wrote to Amnesty International describing a similar experience. Her daughter had been arrested in 1982 when she had been found in possession of leaflets produced by the PMOI. She had been tried by an Islamic Revolutionary Court but never informed of the sentence passed on her. For six years the mother had visited her daughter every two weeks. In early August 1988 her visits were stopped without explanation. In November 1988 she received a telephone call telling her to go to the Islamic Revolutionary Committee office near Beheshteh Zahra cemetery, where she was informed of her daughter's execution. She was instructed not to hold any mourning ceremony and was not informed where the body was buried.

Relatives of prisoners executed in Orumieh Prison in Iranian Kurdistan have described to Amnesty International a form they had to sign when they were summoned to the prison to collect their relatives' belongings. They were told where their relatives were buried, but the authorities had made sure that the 40-day mourning period had elapsed before telling the families about the executions. The form was an undertaking that they would not hold any form of funeral ceremony or erect any memorial on the graves.

Amnesty International has received accounts of similar events in many different prisons in all parts of Iran: in Rasht, Sanandaj, Mashhad, Isfahan and elsewhere. This suggests to Amnesty International that the massacre of political prisoners was a premeditated and coordinated policy which must have been authorized at the highest level of government.

The relatives of prisoners executed during this period have taken to gathering in Beheshteh Zahra cemetery in Tehran on Fridays to commemorate their dead family members. The mother of a 42-year-old man who had been arrested in 1983 and sentenced to 12 years' imprisonment before being executed in Karaj Prison, wrote to her daughter outside Iran about one of these gatherings:

> "On Friday all the mothers along with family members got together and we went to the graveyard. What a day of mourning, it was like Ashura! [A religious festival of particular importance to Shi'a Muslims, commemorating the martyrdom of the Prophet Muhammad's grandson Hossein.] Mothers came with pictures of their sons; one has lost five sons and daughters-in-law. Finally the Committee came and dispersed us."

This gathering of bereaved relatives has reportedly become a regular weekly event in the section of Beheshteh Zahra where political opponents to the government are buried. According to reports from relatives of executed prisoners in Iran, the makeshift monuments erected by the families, which consisted of a few stones and flowers, were removed by the authorities prior to the visit to Tehran by the UN Special Representative on Iran in January 1990. This was apparently an attempt to remove visible evidence of the mass killings from the sight of any possible inspection of the cemetery by the Special Representative.

Amnesty International has also collected accounts of the mass killings as they were witnessed by political prisoners who were in prison at that time. A former prisoner in Dastgerd Prison in Isfahan said that almost every day between August and December 1988 prison guards came to his section of the prison and read out a list of up to 10 names. These people were then taken out of the cell, which generally housed between 150 and 300 people, and never seen again. The prisoners did not know what was happening to those taken away, but the guards said that they were to be executed. Later, prisoners were transferred to Dastgerd Prison from other prisons and news of similar events in these prisons spread among the inmates in Dastgerd.

Prisoners in Gohardasht Prison in Karaj appear to have had a much clearer picture of the events which were taking place. Former prisoners have described to Amnesty International how a commission made up of representatives from the Islamic Revolutionary Courts, the Revolutionary Prosecutor's Office and the Ministry of Intelligence began to subject all political prisoners to a form of retrial in July 1988.

These "retrials" bore little resemblance to judicial proceedings aimed at establishing the guilt or innocence of a defendant with regard to a recognized criminal offence under the law. Instead, they appear to have been formalized interrogation sessions designed to discover the political views of the prisoner in order that prisoners who did not "repent" should be executed -- the punishment of all those who continued to oppose the government.

In Gohardasht Prison those detained for their alleged support for the PMOI were reportedly the first to go before the commission. Other prisoners received information about the "trials" from PMOI prisoners by way of messages tapped on walls in Morse code from room to room inside the prison. According to one prisoner held there at that time, the first question asked by the commission was: "What is your political affiliation?" Those who answered "Mojahedine" were sent to their deaths. The "correct" answer was "monafeqin" (hypocrites). Those prisoners who survived this first phase of interrogation were then subjected to a second series of questions. These included questions such as:

- Are you willing to give an interview on television to condemn and expose the monafeqin?
- Are you willing to fight with the forces of the Islamic Republic against the monafeqin?
- Are you willing to put a noose around the neck of an active member of the monafeqin?
- Are you willing to clear the minefields for the army of the Islamic Republic?

The majority of prisoners were reportedly unwilling to give the desired responses and were consequently sent for execution. Some 200 out of 300 PMOI prisoners in Sections 3 and 4 of Gohardasht Prison were killed following this type of interrogation. The interrogations were reportedly conducted in such a way as to trick prisoners into making statements revealing their opposition to the government.

The prisoners named the interrogators the "Death Commission". It came to Gohardasht Prison three times a week, arriving by helicopter. The same commission was also reportedly at work in Evin Prison.

At the end of August 1988 the "Death Commission" turned its attention to the prisoners from leftist groups held in Gohardasht Prison. These included supporters of the Tudeh Party, various factions of the PFOI, and others. The interrogations followed a similar pattern, with prisoners being asked if they were prepared to make public statements criticizing the political organization with which they had been associated. The leftist prisoners were also asked about their religious faith. They were asked such questions as: Do you pray? Do you read the Qur'an? Did your father read the Qur'an?

One eye-witness of an interrogation in Gohardasht Prison described how he was taken before the "Death Commission" with five other prisoners. The six were asked if they prayed or read the Qur'an: they replied that they did not. They were then asked whether their fathers had read the Qur'an. Four of them answered "yes" and two of them "no". After some discussion between members of the commission, it was decided that those who had not been brought up in a religious family were not as guilty as those whose parents were religious, because the former group had not been brought up as believers. Consequently, the two men whose fathers had not prayed were spared, but the four others were executed.

According to another eye-witness account of this period in Gohardasht Prison, the decisions about which prisoners were to be executed and which spared were arbitrary in the extreme. Some prisoners who had been sentenced to death by the commission were spared because prison guards sent prisoners whom they disliked to be executed in their place. There was also a great deal of confusion as prisoners were transferred from different prisons, and from section to section within the prison. As a result of such confusion, prisoners were sometimes executed by mistake.

The same eye-witness estimates that out of 900 PMOI and 600 leftist prisoners in Gohardasht Prison at the beginning of the summer of 1988, 600 PMOI prisoners and 200 leftist prisoners were executed. In Evin Prison, where the execution of prisoners was going on simultaneously, the proportion of executions carried out from the total population of political prisoners was much higher. One reason suggested for this is that in Evin there was no way for prisoners to communicate with each other, so they were unable to prepare answers to questions put to them by the "Death Commission" as prisoners in Gohardasht had done.

A similar pattern of purposeful mass killing of political opponents, beginning with the PMOI but encompassing alleged supporters of other opposition groups, took place in dozens of other prisons around the country in the second half of 1988. Among others, Amnesty International has received reports of hundreds of executions of prisoners from Kurdish opposition groups in Orumieh Prison, and of 50 being executed in Sanandaj.

Ayatollah Montazeri's letters to Ayatollah Khomeini in July 1988 reportedly criticized many of the aspects of the mass executions identified by former prisoners. Ayatollah Montazeri commented on the arbitrary way in which life and death decisions were taken:

> "He [Ayatollah Montazeri] cited the case of a provincial
> mullah who had complained that a prisoner who had fully
> recanted was executed anyway. The prisoner, who was not

named, said in response to the tribunal questions that he
was ready to publicly condemn his past opposition, and to go
to the Gulf War front as well. But when he refused to
declare his readiness to go to the minefields, the tribunal
decided he had not truly changed and had him executed."
(Reuters, 29 March 1989)

In a later letter, dated 15 August 1988, Ayatollah Montazeri is
reported to have demanded of the Minister of Intelligence, the Prosecutor
General and the Chief Justice: "On what criteria are you now executing
people who have not been sentenced to death?"(Reuters, 29 March 1989)

Ayatollah Montazeri's letters show that there was awareness at the
highest level of the government that "thousands" of summary executions were
taking place without regard to constitutional and judicial procedures. The
authorities were therefore either unable to prevent these mass killings
from taking place, or they did not wish to do so.

The mass killing of political prisoners appears to have stopped at the
beginning of 1989, when several hundred repentant political prisoners were
included in amnesties to mark the 10th anniversary of the Islamic
Republic's foundation in February 1979. Those who were released had to
sign statements denouncing their earlier political activities. They were
further obliged to pledge large sums of money, or in some cases the deeds
of the family house, against their future good conduct and non-involvement
in opposition politics. The amnesty brought to an end a period of six to
eight months which saw a massive reduction in the numbers of political
prisoners in Iran through executions.

Since February 1989 sporadic reports of executions of the government's
political opponents in Iran have been received by Amnesty International.
Some of these executions have taken place in public. For example, in March
1989 Mohammad and Saeed Khan Naroui were hanged from a crane in Abbas Ali
Square in Gorgan. They had been imprisoned since 1984 for "inciting the
people to revolt".

On 28 March 1990 the execution of two men described as "bandits" was
announced by the Islamic Republic News Agency. Abbas Raisi and Ahmad Jangi
Razhi were found guilty by the Islamic Revolutionary Court in Zahedan of
"collaborating with bandits and counter-revolutionaries in the Baluchistan
area" (BBC Summary of World Broadcasts, 30 March 1990)

Secret executions of political prisoners have also been reported.
Following the assassination in July 1989 of the leader of the KDPI, Abdul
Rahman Ghassemlou, in circumstances which suggest the involvement of the
Iranian Government, resistance to the government, including armed
opposition, is reported to have been stepped up in Iranian Kurdistan. The
authorities are reported to have responded by executing Kurdish prisoners
in Sanandaj and Orumieh Prisons. Executions of Kurdish opponents to the
government have continued in 1990.

Other political prisoners are reported to have been executed ostensibly as common criminals; they were among the hundreds of drug-traffickers and other convicted criminals executed in public in 1989 and 1990. For example, it was announced that 79 drug-traffickers were executed in different cities on 17 August 1989. Among them were Mohammad Younesi, executed in Hamadan; Mohammad Gholi Ebrahimi, executed in Rasht; Bijan Biglari, executed in Kermanshah (Bakhtaran); and Bahram Kazemi and Massoud Sabet, executed in Shiraz. All these were reportedly political prisoners. Amnesty International has received no response to its requests for information from the Iranian authorities about the offences of which these prisoners were convicted.

1.3 Extrajudicial Executions

Amnesty International opposes unreservedly the extrajudicial killing of any individual on political grounds by governments. Since 1987 a number of Iranian opposition personalities in exile have been attacked, apparently by agents of the Iranian Government. In some cases the attacks have resulted in the deaths of prominent individuals opposed to the government's policies.

For example, there were reports of Iranian Government involvement in 1987 in the killing of Hamid Chitgar in Vienna in May and various incidents in July: a bomb attack on the car of Amir Parviz in London in which he was seriously injured; the killing of Muhammad Hassan Mansuri and the wounding of an Iraqi diplomat, Behnam Fadhel, in Istanbul and armed attacks on a number of Iranian exiles in Quetta and Karachi.

In 1989 there was a further cluster of killings of opposition personalities in circumstances which suggested the complicity of the Iranian authorities. On 4 June Atayollah Byahmadi, a former colonel in the Shah's Intelligence Service, was shot dead in his hotel room in Dubai, in the United Arab Emirates. On 13 July Dr Abdul Rahman Ghassemlou, leader of the KDPI, was killed in a Vienna apartment together with two companions. He was in Austria taking part in negotiations with representatives of the Iranian Government. In November the Austrian authorities issued arrest warrants for three suspects: they included Iranian Government agents who had left Austria or gone into hiding in the Iranian Embassy in Vienna after the killings. In August Bahman Javadi, a member of the Central Committee of the Communist Party of Iran, was killed and a companion seriously wounded when unidentified gunmen attacked them in a street in Cyprus. Bahman Javadi had apparently gone to Cyprus for a personal reunion with his mother, whom he had not seen for seven years.

In April 1990 Dr Kazem Rajavi, representative of the PMOI in Geneva and brother of the PMOI's leader, Massoud Rajavi, was shot and killed while driving his car near his home just outside Geneva. A Swiss judge investigating the murder said that preliminary investigations indicated "the direct involvement in the murder of one or more Iranian official services" and the implication in the murder of at least 13 Iranian citizens enjoying diplomatic or other official status.

The Iranian authorities may not have been involved in all these killings and attempted killings. Some of the victims had other enemies who may have wished to see them dead. However, in the killings of Dr Ghassemlou and his companions, and of Dr Rajavi, police investigations have revealed clear evidence pointing to the involvement of the Iranian Government.

Other incidents have exposed the involvement of Iranian Government officials in illegal activity outside Iran directed against political opponents. For example, in November 1988 Iranian diplomats in Turkey were caught with a kidnapped Iranian political refugee bound and gagged in the boot of their diplomatic car. They were apparently attempting to return him to Iran against his will.

Following reports of political killings outside Iran, Amnesty International has written to the Iranian authorities urging them to condemn publicly the practice of extrajudicial executions and to make clear to all government officials and representatives in Iran and abroad that such killings will not be tolerated.

Amnesty International includes in its definition of extrajudicial executions the killing of specific individuals which can be reasonably assumed to be the result of government policy at any level. For this reason it has been concerned by the Iranian Government's continuing endorsement of threats against the life of Salman Rushdie, the British author of The Satanic Verses. In February 1989 Ayatollah Khomeini issued a fatwa (religious edict) to the effect that it was the duty of Muslims everywhere to put the novelist to death, as he judged the book to be blasphemous. Amnesty International is not aware of any direct attempt by agents of the Iranian Government to kill Salman Rushdie, but the repeated endorsement of Ayatollah Khomeini's edict by numerous government authorities in Iran indicates that the Iranian authorities would condone his extrajudicial execution. Amnesty International has repeatedly called on the Iranian authorities to withdraw their support for any threat to Salman Rushdie's life.

1.4 Relevant International Standards

Amnesty International is opposed to the death penalty in all cases. It regards the death penalty as a violation of the right to life and the most extreme form of cruel, inhuman and degrading punishment.

Article 3 of the Universal Declaration of Human Rights states: "Everyone has the right to life." Article 5 states: "No-one shall be subjected to torture or to cruel, inhuman or degrading treatment or punishment."

In its resolution 32/61 of 1977 the UN General Assembly reaffirmed that the goal for all states should be the progressive abolition of the death penalty.

Provisions in the Law of Hodoud and Qisas do not conform to international standards governing the use of the death penalty in countries which have not yet abolished it.

Article 6(2) of the ICCPR states that in countries which have not yet abolished the death penalty it should be imposed only for "the most serious crimes". The Human Rights Committee has explained in its General Comment 6(16) that "the most serious crimes" must be read "restrictively" and that the death penalty should be "a quite exceptional measure". Safeguards Guaranteeing Protection of the Rights of Those Facing the Death Penalty, adopted by the UN Economic and Social Council in 1984 (ECOSOC Safeguards), annexed to Resolution 1984/50, and endorsed by the Seventh UN Congress on the Prevention of Crime and the Treatment of Offenders in 1985, make it clear that the scope of capital crimes "should not go beyond intentional crimes, with lethal or other extremely grave consequences". In Iran the death penalty is applied so frequently and for such a wide range of offences that it clearly cannot be considered to be applied as "a quite exceptional measure".

Article 6(2) of the ICCPR prohibits executions which are "contrary to the provisions of the present Covenant", thus incorporating the procedural guarantees for fair trial in Article 14.

General Assembly Resolution 35/172 (1980) urges Member States to respect, as a minimum, the guarantees in Articles 6, 14 and 15 of the ICCPR, and:

> "to review their legal rules and practices so as to guarantee the most careful legal procedures and the greatest possible safeguards for the accused in capital cases."

The ECOSOC Safeguards require the highest possible standard of proof in death penalty cases and all possible safeguards to ensure a fair trial, at least equal to those contained in Article 14 of the ICCPR.

In Iran, violations of these standards are widespread (see Chapter Two).

ECOSOC Safeguard 9 requires that "[w]here capital punishment occurs, it shall be carried out so as to inflict the minimum possible suffering." This safeguard is flouted by such execution methods as stoning to death, which are designed to inflict the maximum possible suffering.

Under the Law of Hodoud and Qisas there do not appear to be any limitations on the execution of those who have committed offences when under 18 years of age, contrary to Article 6(5) of the ICCPR, which specifies: "Sentence of death shall not be imposed for crimes committed by persons below eighteen years of age".

The UN has shown continued concern about the problem of summary and arbitrary executions as reflected in the ECOSOC Safeguards and in the

Principles for the Effective Prevention and Investigation of Extra-legal, Arbitrary and Summary Executions, adopted by the ECOSOC in Resolution 1989/65 on 24 May 1989.

1.5 Amnesty International's Recommendations

The record of executions from 1987 to 1990 reinforces the urgency of the recommendations included in Amnesty International's 1987 report, which should be implemented without delay:

"Amnesty International respectfully urges the Government of the Islamic Republic of Iran to demonstrate its respect for the inherent right to life by putting an immediate end to executions.

"Pending the carrying out of such a decision, Amnesty International would draw the attention of the Government of the Islamic Republic of Iran to Resolution 35/172 adopted by the UN General Assembly on 15 December 1980, which urged all Member States:

"1 (a) To respect as a minimum standard the contents of the provisions of articles 6, 14 and 15 of the International Covenant on Civil and Political Rights and, where necessary, to review their legal rules and practices so as to guarantee the most careful legal procedures and the greatest possible safeguards for the accused in capital cases;

"(b) To examine carefully the possibility of making automatic the appeal procedure, where it exists, in cases of death sentences, as well as the consideration of an amnesty, pardon or commutation in these cases;

"(c) To provide that no death sentence shall be carried out until the procedures of appeal and pardon have been terminated and, in any case, not until a reasonable time after passing of the sentence in the court in the first instance."

CHAPTER TWO: <u>UNFAIR TRIALS</u>

Many hundreds of political prisoners and others held as criminal suspects have been sentenced to death and executed after unfair trials in Iran. They were tried and sentenced by Islamic Revolutionary Courts or Penal Court (One), in both of which trials fall short of international standards for fair trial.

The failure of the Iranian judicial system to provide adequate safeguards for defendants facing trial in capital cases, and in trials of political prisoners, is one of the fundamental reasons for the prevalence of large-scale human rights abuses in Iran.

Iran's judicial system is under review at the present time. Amnesty International hopes that the opportunity will be taken to bring court procedures into conformity with international human rights standards.

2.1   <u>The Structure of the Judiciary</u>

Before describing the structure of the Iranian judicial system, a note of caution must be added about the extent to which proceedings involving offenders, particularly in political cases, have followed the procedures provided for by this structure. Moreover, the government has created additional types of court which appear to operate outside the confines of this judicial system.

Because Amnesty International attaches great importance to the issue of fair trial, it has frequently requested information from the Iranian authorities about procedures followed in individual cases and about the system in general. The authorities have never replied to these inquiries other than by blanket statements that all trials are fair. In the absence of any detailed response, therefore, the following description of the judicial system is based on an analysis of the relevant Iranian legislation and on the reported statements of Iranian judicial authorities, as well as the evidence of individual case histories.

2.1.1   <u>The Courts</u>

The judicial system provides for five types of court: General Courts dealing with civil matters; Special Civil Courts dealing with family law and various other private cases; Penal Courts divided into No.One and No.Two Divisions; Military Courts and Islamic Revolutionary Courts.

Cases of concern to Amnesty International have mainly been heard in Penal Court (One) or in Islamic Revolutionary Courts. However, there are at least two other types of courts which have passed verdicts of concern to Amnesty International. In early 1989 Special Judicial Committees were established by the Supreme Judicial Council, on the authority of the Leader of the Islamic Republic, Ayatollah Khomeini. They were empowered to investigate complaints directly and issue sentences, including the death penalty, with no apparent reference to the existing judicial structures. A further judicial body with power to issue death sentences without reference to other judicial structures is a special court for clerics which is accountable to the Leader of the Islamic Republic.

There is also a Supreme Court in Tehran, with a branch in Qom, charged with establishing unity of practice in the adjudication process.

Ayatollah Yazdi, the Head of the Judiciary, was reported to have said in an interview with <u>Keyhan Havai</u> newspaper on 24 July 1990, that Parliament was studying a bill for the formation of a unified court system aimed at facilitating central control over the judicial process.

2.1.2 Judicial Authorities

Among the constitutional amendments adopted by referendum in July 1989 was the establishment of a new post, Head of the Judiciary. This new authority took over the role of the Supreme Judicial Council -- that is, to bear responsibility for the appointment and dismissal of judges, the drafting of bills of law to be considered by the Islamic Consultative Assembly, and the drafting of guidelines for the enforcement of legislation by the courts. The first incumbent of this post, appointed directly by the Leader of the Islamic Republic, was Ayatollah Mohammad Yazdi. The Head of the Judiciary appoints the Prosecutor General and the President of the Supreme Court. The judiciary is independent of the Minister of Justice, who is in charge of the administrative organization of the courts. The Minister of Justice responds to questions about the judiciary in the Islamic Consultative Assembly, providing a constitutional shield for the judiciary against political pressure from the legislature.

2.2 Procedures of Concern to Amnesty International

2.2.1 Penal Court (One)

Penal Court (One) has jurisdiction over serious criminal cases in which the sentences which may be imposed are the death penalty (including stoning to death), amputation, imprisonment for over 10 years, or fines in excess of 20,000 toumans.

Penal Courts (One) are presided over by a judge or an alternate judge; both of whom are competent to make rulings. If the judge is not a fully qualified religious judge (<u>mojtahid</u>), an assessor may help by giving an opinion on the case before the presiding judge rules on it.

No actual judgment is passed by Penal Court (One). The criminal court sends its views on how the case should be resolved to the Supreme Court. If the Supreme Court approves the recommendation then Penal Court (One) issues the sentence. If the Supreme Court disagrees with the recommendation then the case is referred to a second Penal Court (One). If the dispute continues a plenary session of the Supreme Court meets to issue a binding judgment which resolves the matter.

According to Article 14(3)(d) of the ICCPR, everyone is entitled "to be tried in his presence, and to defend himself in person or through legal assistance of his own choosing." The procedures followed in cases before Penal Court (One) do not appear to provide defendants with the right to defend themselves during the review of their cases by the Supreme Court, which would appear to be an integral part of their trial.

According to the report of the Special Representative of the UN Human Rights Commission (UN document E/CN.4/1990/24) who visited Tehran in January 1990, the Special Representative was assured in meetings with senior judicial officials that the right of appeal is recognized in all cases. Once the judgment is handed down, which occurs only after the Supreme Court has approved the verdict of Penal Court (One), the defendant is said to have the right to appeal to the Supreme Court.

Amnesty International is concerned about the procedures as described above as they appear to involve the Supreme Court issuing a verdict in a given case as part of the trial by the court of first instance, and provide for appeal only to the same Supreme Court which has already issued a ruling on the case. These procedures would appear to fall short of the requirements of Article 14(5) of the ICCPR (see page 29) and do not appear to take account of the fair and public hearing requirements of Article 14(1), which the Human Rights Committee, established under the ICCPR to monitor its implementation, indicated in its General Comment 13(21) apply to appeals.

2.2.2   Islamic Revolutionary Courts

The majority of death sentences in Iran in recent years have been imposed by Islamic Revolutionary Courts. In 1989 over 1,000 people were convicted of drug-trafficking offences by such courts and subsequently executed. The number of executions carried out for drug-trafficking offences remained high in 1990 with over 100 such executions reported in the first six months of the year. Revolutionary Courts also have jurisdiction over a range of offences which have led to the imprisonment and execution of political prisoners, including prisoners of conscience.

Islamic Revolutionary Courts were created as an emergency measure after the 1979 revolution, mainly to try the cases of people arrested in connection with activities for the deposed government. They have since become institutionalized. In March 1990 the Prosecutor General, Hojatoleslam Reyshahri, is reported to have responded to private calls for their abolition by saying: "Islamic Revolutionary Courts must be retained as long as the revolution prevails." (Iran Focus, March 1990)

The Human Rights Committee has noted the existence in many countries of military or special courts which try civilians, but has stated that the trying of civilians before such courts:

"...could present serious problems as far as the equitable, impartial and independent administration of justice is concerned and that the International Covenant on Civil and Political Rights clearly indicates that the trying of civilians before such courts should be very exceptional and take place under conditions which genuinely afford the full guarantees stipulated under Article 14." (General Comment 13(21) by the Human Rights Committee)

The jurisdiction of Islamic Revolutionary Courts covers:

"1. All crimes against internal or external security, <u>Moharabeh</u>, (enmity to God) and corruption on earth.

2. Attempts on the life of political personalities.

3. All crimes related to narcotics and smuggling.

4. Murder, killing, imprisoning and torturing for the purpose of consolidating the Pahlavi regime and suppressing the struggle of the people of Iran whether as an associate or as an accomplice.

5. Plunder of the public treasury.

6. Profiteering and hoarding of general provisions." (Approved in May 1983 and published in Official Gazette No. 11139)

The Administrative Regulations Governing the Revolutionary Courts and Public Prosecutor's Offices which came into force in 1979 stipulate that an Islamic Revolutionary Court should consist of three members: the court should be presided over by a religious judge, one of the other two members should be a judge from the Ministry of Justice and the third an individual with a reputation for trustworthiness. In practice, eye-witnesses have informed Amnesty International that such courts have consisted of only one judge who has discharged his duties in a summary fashion, with trial hearings lasting only a few minutes.

While the above-mentioned Administrative Regulations refer to the defendant being represented by a lawyer, Amnesty International is not aware that any defendant in a political trial has ever enjoyed this basic right, guaranteed by Article 14(3)(d) of the ICCPR and the Body of Principles for the Protection of All Persons under Any Form of Detention or Imprisonment, as well as Principle 35 of the Constitution of the Islamic Republic of Iran.

Trials before Islamic Revolutionary Courts have usually taken place in secret inside prisons, with the defendant often being unaware that the proceedings were a trial rather than an interrogation session. Charges have not been made clear to the defendant before the trial, contrary to Article

14(3)(a) of the ICCPR, which requires that everyone charged with a criminal offence is entitled: "to be informed promptly and in detail in a language which he understands of the nature and the cause of the charge against him". Moreover, contrary to Article 14(3)(b) of the ICCPR, which requires that persons charged with criminal offences have "adequate time and facilities" to prepare their defence, defendants are given no opportunity to prepare a defence of any kind.

Political prisoners may be held in indefinite pre-trial detention. This is contrary to Article 32 of the Constitution of the Islamic Republic of Iran (see Chapter Three below). Amnesty International has received many reports of such prisoners being subjected to torture and ill-treatment during such periods of detention in order to force them to confess to offences. These confessions have then led to their conviction by Islamic Revolutionary Courts despite a statutory and constitutional prohibition on the use of torture to extract confessions.

Note 2 of Article 11 of the Administrative Regulations makes it clear that: "Judgments of the Revolutionary Court shall be final and no revision be made thereon." Thus the regulations do not provide for any right of appeal against verdict or sentence. The failure to provide for an appeal contravenes Article 14(5) of the ICCPR, which provides: "Everyone convicted of a crime shall have the right to his conviction and sentence being reviewed by a higher tribunal according to law." The Safeguards Guaranteeing Protection of the Rights of those Facing the Death Penalty, adopted by the ECOSOC in 1984, require that: "Anyone sentenced to death shall have the right to appeal to a court of higher jurisdiction, and steps should be taken to ensure that such appeals become mandatory."

The picture which emerges is one of arbitrary procedures by a court system which does not comply with either the requirements of domestic legislation and regulations, nor minimum international standards for fair trial.

In its 1987 report Amnesty International expressed particular concern about the conduct of trials before Islamic Revolutionary Courts, and indicated that the Administrative Regulations Governing Revolutionary Courts contained inadequate provisions for ensuring fair trial. Since then, Amnesty International is not aware of any amendment to these regulations which might have alleviated these concerns.

Article 14 of the ICCPR, ratified by Iran in 1975, is a primary human rights instrument in the field of fair trial. Its provisions prescribe the minimum standards to which all trials should conform. Paragraph 1 stipulates that "everyone shall be entitled to a fair and public hearing by a competent, independent and impartial tribunal established by law". Trials by Islamic Revolutionary Courts, particularly in political cases, take place in camera with no provision for attendance by members of the family or defence counsel. Paragraph 1 also requires that the judgment issued in a criminal case should be made public. Amnesty International is aware of numerous cases in Iran where this has not been done, and where even the defendants themselves have not been informed of the sentence passed on them. The Special Representative of the UN Human Rights Commission in his February 1990 Report (cited above) described in paragraph 213 his meeting with "an experienced lawyer". The lawyer said that in cases where death sentences were passed by Islamic Revolutionary Courts "the defendant was never informed of his condemnation."

Paragraph 2 of Article 14 states: "Everyone charged with a criminal offence shall have the right to be presumed innocent until proved guilty according to law."

Dozens of former political prisoners have described the extremely summary nature of their trials by Islamic Revolutionary Courts, which lasted only a few minutes. Such summary proceedings fail to ensure the presumption of the defendants' innocence, which the Human Rights Committee, in its General Comment 13(21), has declared "is fundamental to the protection of human rights".

Other factors militate against the presumption of innocence in trials before Islamic Revolutionary Courts. The most draconian punishments have been meted out by these courts in cases related to activities by proscribed opposition groups, and to drug-trafficking offences. The government has waged a sustained campaign of vilification against opposition groups, particularly those which have resorted to armed opposition such as the PMOI. Many government leaders have made public statements calling for PMOI supporters to be killed without mercy. The level of this kind of official propaganda may undermine the right of those accused of allegiance to such groups to be presumed innocent and may make lawyers reluctant to defend those accused, for fear of also becoming suspect.

In the case of drug-trafficking offences the official pressure to convict and execute large numbers of drug-traffickers (see Chapter One) must detract from the presumption of innocence of anyone accused of such offences. The fervour of these campaigns would appear to contravene the Body of Principles on the Independence of the Judiciary which states, in Principle 4, that "there shall not be any inappropriate or unwarranted interference with the judicial process."

Article 14(3) of the ICCPR provides various minimum guarantees which appear to be absent in trials before Islamic Revolutionary Courts. These include: the right to be informed promptly and in detail of the nature and cause of the charge; the right to adequate time and facilities for the preparation of defence; the right to legal assistance; the right to examine prosecution witnesses and to bring witnesses in defence; and the right not to be compelled to testify against oneself or to confess guilt.

A recent case involving 10 people who, according to an Islamic Republic News Agency report of 26 April 1990, were "arrested for spying for the USA" is a typical example of the process experienced by defendants in hundreds of political trials.

The 10 were arrested at the end of 1988. No reason was given for their detention, and their families were not informed of their whereabouts for many months. The prisoners were held in incommunicado detention until about August 1989 when family visits were permitted for the first time. Soon afterwards several Iranian newspapers reported that the prisoners had confessed to charges of "spying for the USA." Their trial was held in secret in Evin Prison. The families were informed after the trial that their relatives had been sentenced to death. No appeal against verdict or sentence appears to have been permitted. The prisoners had not been granted access to a lawyer during their trial, or at any time during their imprisonment. Amnesty International has since learned that at least one of those convicted has been executed.

This pattern whereby suspected political opponents of the government, including prisoners of conscience, have been held in indefinite pre-trial detention, tortured and forced to confess, and then sentenced after a summary trial, at which no defence lawyer was present and at which no defence witnesses were permitted, repeats itself time and time again in the testimonies of former Iranian political prisoners obtained by Amnesty International.

Article 14(5) of the ICCPR requires that, "(E)veryone convicted of a crime shall have the right to his conviction and sentence being reviewed by a higher tribunal according to law." There is considerable doubt about how far this requirement is satisfied in cases tried by Islamic Revolutionary Courts. Although the Administrative Regulations Governing the Revolutionary Courts and the Public Prosecutor's Offices clearly rule out the possibility of judgments by Islamic Revolutionary Courts being revised in any way, senior judicial officials have referred on a number of occasions to the availability of a review of Revolutionary Court verdicts by a special division of the Supreme Court. The President of the Supreme Court, Ayatollah Moghtadaei, told the UN Special Representative that "the right of appeal is recognized and no exception is made in cases under the jurisdiction of the revolutionary courts." (UN document E/CN.4/1990/24, para 97) Amnesty International has not been able to establish what law provides for such appeals and has been unable to document any cases in which such appeals were heard.

Speaking about Ayatollah Khomeini's judicial legacy in May 1990 the Head of the Judiciary, Ayatollah Yazdi, remarked that on the basis of Ayatollah Khomeini's writings on the subject, "...it is not permissible for the verdicts issued by qualified jurists (mojtahedine) to be reviewed or subject to appeal." (Ettela'at, 30 May 1990)

The "experienced lawyer" who spoke to the UN Special Representative during the same visit is reported to have said that:

"Before Islamic Revolution[ary] Courts no legal rep[r]esentation was possible and no appeals were admitted. In cases of death sentences passed by these courts the defendant was never informed of his condemnation. Such sentences were reviewed by the competent section of the Supreme Court without the defendant's knowledge that he had been sentenced to death and without any further hearings." (UN document E/CN.4/1990/24, para 213)

The "right of appeal" referred to by Ayatollah Moghtadaei is probably a reference to the High Court at Qom; this court became operative a few months after the 1979 revolution on the instruction of the Leader of the Islamic Republic. Its jurisdiction was to review the judgments of Islamic Revolutionary Courts where the punishment passed on the accused was the death sentence or confiscation of property. The composition and procedures of this court were never made public, and there is no indication that political prisoners have ever had access to it. If reviews by the court are carried out as described by the "experienced lawyer", it is of little use to the defendant as a safeguard. Moreover, it denies the defendant the fair and public hearing guarantees which the Human Rights Committee has made clear in its General Comment 13(21) apply to appellate review.

Article 6(4) of the ICCPR states that: "Anyone sentenced to death shall have the right to seek pardon or commutation of the sentence." The Safeguards Guaranteeing Protection of the Rights of Those Facing the Death Penalty, adopted by the ECOSOC, contain the same guarantee under Safeguard 7. The failure to inform a defendant that he or she has been sentenced to death effectively deprives the defendant of the right to seek pardon or commutation.

Islamic Revolutionary Courts continue to sanction dozens of executions every month in circumstances where miscarriages of justice would appear to be inevitable. Hundreds of political prisoners, including prisoners of conscience, are serving prison sentences imposed after unfair trials before such courts.

2.2.3 Other Special Courts

It is notable that the outstanding incident of gross human rights abuse in Iran during the period since 1987 -- the massacre of thousands of political prisoners during the latter part of 1988 -- took place without any apparent reference to established judicial procedures.

Impatience with judicial procedures -- even the hasty procedures of the Islamic Revolutionary Courts -- which were perceived to stand in the way of the expeditious punishment of offenders led, in the early part of 1989, to the establishment of Special Judicial Committees. These were empowered to carry out inquiries and enforce sentences without reference to the competent courts.

The President of the Supreme Judicial Council, Ayatollah Ardebili, described a system whereby a representative of the Leader of the Islamic Republic "from outside the maze of the judicial system" could "hold an immediate trial" and bring cases to an end "in a matter of three, four or five days." (BBC Summary of World Broadcasts, 23 January 1989)

The measures to speed up the judicial process emerged as a result of political pressure, led by Ayatollah Khomeini. One hundred and ninety members of the Islamic Consultative Assembly supported a resolution criticizing the judiciary and calling on it to speed up its procedures in accordance with the Leader's instructions on 18 January 1989.

One result of these moves has been a massive increase in the numbers of executions of convicted criminal offenders. Amnesty International's recorded figures for such executions rose from 148 in 1988 to over 1,500 in 1989. It is not clear how many of these occurred after trials conducted by Special Judicial Committees, but the figures suggest that such safeguards as may have existed for defendants in the past were reduced yet further. In particular, the right of each defendant "to have adequate time and facilities for the preparation of his defence" must have been undermined by procedures whereby officials were instructed to complete cases, from arrest to execution, within a few days. In October 1989 Parliament sent a note of thanks to the Head of the Judiciary following a report that a man accused of the murder of nine people was arrested, tried, convicted and executed within 24 hours in Delfan, Lorestan Province. The Supreme Judicial Council proposed, in early 1989, that new General Courts should be established to speed up the criminal justice system, but in July 1990 this proposal was still under discussion by Parliament and no formal addition to the court system had been made.

Speaking in Khoramabad, in Lorestan Province, on 27 November 1989 the Head of the Judiciary, Ayatollah Yazdi, said:

> "General policies of the judiciary are based, as far as possible, upon eliminating the interval between the committing of a crime and the punishment of the convict, so that the convict is punished as soon as possible." (Keyhan newspaper, Tehran, 28 November 1989)

Ayatollah Yazdi added:

> "I have emphasized many times that care must be taken to ensure that speed is not achieved at the expense of accuracy, or at the expense of the rights of the defendant."

Amnesty International welcomes Ayatollah Yazdi's stated concern to ensure that judicial procedures uphold the rights of defendants. However, the Head of the Judiciary's statement indicated no steps which had been or were to be taken to safeguard such rights, and Amnesty International is not aware of any such measures. Indeed, political pressure to speed up the judicial process has led to a further deterioration in judicial safeguards. Trials which begin almost immediately after arrest and are completed in a few days cannot possibly provide defendants with the rights to which they are entitled. Rather than succumb to political pressure for speedy punishments as a means of setting an example, the judiciary should uphold the rights of defendants and ensure that they receive fair trials. Principle 2 of the Basic Principles on the Independence of the Judiciary states:

"2. The judiciary shall decide matters before them impartially, on the basis of facts and in accordance with the law, without any restrictions, improper influences, inducements, pressures, threats or interferences, direct or indirect, from any quarter or for any reason."

The establishment of special courts apparently outside the legally constituted judicial system can only erode further the principle of the rule of law at the expense of the rights of defendants. Principle 5 of the Basic Principles on the Independence of the Judiciary states:

"5. Everyone shall have the right to be tried by ordinary courts or tribunals using established legal procedures. Tribunals that do not use the duly established procedures of the legal process shall not be created to displace the jurisdiction belonging to the ordinary courts or judicial tribunals."

Speaking about the proposed new General Courts, Ayatollah Yazdi was reported in Keyhan newspaper on 16 December 1989 as saying that these courts were to be based on Islamic principles, in contrast to the existing Penal Courts which were based on the French system. In the General Courts, Ayatollah Yazdi said, the judge would also assume the role of the Public Prosecutor. By doing so, however, the judge would violate the fundamental guarantee of "a fair and public hearing by a competent, independent and impartial tribunal established by law", set forth in Article 14(1) of the ICCPR and the requirement regarding independence and impartiality set out in Principle 2 of the Basic Principles on the Independence of the Judiciary cited above.

In its December 1989 edition, the monthly journal Iran Focus observed that the death penalty for murder and drug-trafficking, stoning for adultery, and amputations were being carried out more often as a result of changes in the judiciary.

Other courts which exist outside the official judicial system are the special courts for clerics. It was these courts which were responsible for the death sentences in late 1987 passed on Mehdi Hashemi, a relative of the then designated successor to Ayatollah Khomeini, Ayatollah Montazeri, and two of his associates. The most recent victims of this court were Sharifeddin Mashkoun and Abdolreza Hejazi, who were executed in April or May 1990. Amnesty International is not aware of the procedures followed in these courts, but is concerned that they appear to have been used as a means of resolving factional struggles within the clerical leadership rather than as courts of law.

Iran continues to have a judicial system which offers little protection to political prisoners or to those on trial for offences which carry the death penalty. Fundamental safeguards have been disregarded, most flagrantly when the government proceeded unchecked to kill its political opponents in the latter part of 1988, but also in the formation of special courts.

A strong and independent judiciary is an important guardian of human rights. To achieve a lasting improvement in Iran's human rights record, all special courts should be abolished, including the Islamic Revolutionary Courts. Proposals to merge the various courts in a more centralized system, referred to by the Head of the Judiciary in July 1990 (Keyhan Havai newspaper, 24 July 1990), would be welcome if this facilitated the provision of fair trials in accordance with the law. The system should be brought into conformity with international human rights standards such as Articles 6 and 14 of the ICCPR, the Basic Principles on the Independence of the Judiciary, and the Body of Principles for the Protection of All Persons under any Form of Detention or Imprisonment.

2.2.4 Amnesty International's Recommendations

Amnesty International's key recommendations in its 1987 report continue today to remain valid:

> "C.1 Amnesty International is disturbed by the numerous and consistent reports of summary trials of political prisoners, particularly those trials taking place before Islamic Revolutionary Courts. The organization respectfully recommends an urgent review of all stages of the judicial process in order to integrate into them all the basic safeguards established in Article 14 of the ICCPR. Amnesty International considers such a measure would be an important step towards the protection of prisoners from summary and unfair trials.

> "Amnesty International therefore respectfully draws the attention of the Government of the Islamic Republic of Iran to General Comment 3(21) by the Human Rights Committee on Article 14 of the ICCPR, which notes the existence in many countries of military or special courts which try civilians, but indicates that such proceedings 'should be very exceptional and take place under conditions which genuinely afford the full guarantees stipulated in Article 14'.

> "Amnesty International is deeply concerned about the conduct of trials before Islamic Revolutionary Courts. It considers that the Administrative Regulations Governing Revolutionary Courts and Public Prosecutors Offices contain inadequate provisions to ensure fair trials, and it is Amnesty International's experience that even safeguards established by law are not maintained. Amnesty International understands that these courts were created as a temporary measure only and recommends that consideration now be given to abolishing them so as to consolidate all judicial proceedings in one system, which should supply all the safeguards necessary for a fair trial. Amnesty International respectfully recommends that such steps be taken into consideration in the course of making any review of existing legislation... .

"3 Finally, in recommending that all provisions of Article 14 of the ICCPR be legally enforced without delay, as a minimum step towards protection from unfair trial, Amnesty International respectfully recalls the Human Rights Committee's General Comment 3(13) on the implementation of the Covenant:

"Implementation does not depend solely on constitutional or legislative enactments, which in themselves are often not per se sufficient. The Committee considers it necessary to draw the attention of States Parties to the fact that their obligation under the Covenant is not confined to the respect of human rights, but that States Parties have also undertaken to ensure the enjoyment of these rights to all individuals under their jurisdiction. This aspect calls for specific activities by the States Parties to enable individuals to enjoy their rights."

Public execution in Tabriz in 1989. The bodies of nine prisoners dangle from a crane mounted on the back of a lorry which has been used as a gibbet to hang them. Other prisoners were hanged at the same time from a crane on a second lorry, parked alongside. After executions, these portable gibbets may be driven through the streets with the bodies still hanging from them.

"A depraved man stoned to death in Mashhad" was the caption of this photograph published in a local newspaper, Khorassan, on 18 January 1990. The Islamic Penal Code of Iran states that male victims of stoning should be buried in a pit up to the waist, female victims up to the chest. Amnesty International has recorded dozens of stonings in Iran since 1987.

Dr Kazem Rajavi killed near Geneva in April 1990. Investigations by the Swiss authorities indicated the direct involvement in the murder of one or more Iranian official services. Dr Kazem Rajavi's car after the shooting. He was killed while driving near his home.

Dr Abdul Rahman Ghassemlou, leader of the Kurdish Democratic Party of Iran, killed in Vienna in July 1989. In November 1989 the Austrian authorities issued arrest warrants for three suspects: they included Iranian Government agents who had left Austria or gone into hiding in the Iranian Embassy in Vienna after the killing.

Ezzatollah Sahabi

Hossein Bani Assadi

Reza Sadr

Hashem Sabbaghian

Ali Ardalan

Signatories to an open letter addressed to President Rafsanjani:
prisoners of conscience arrested in June 1990.

Mariam Firouz, a prisoner of conscience since 1983, now over 70 years old.

Women Prisoners in Evin Prison.

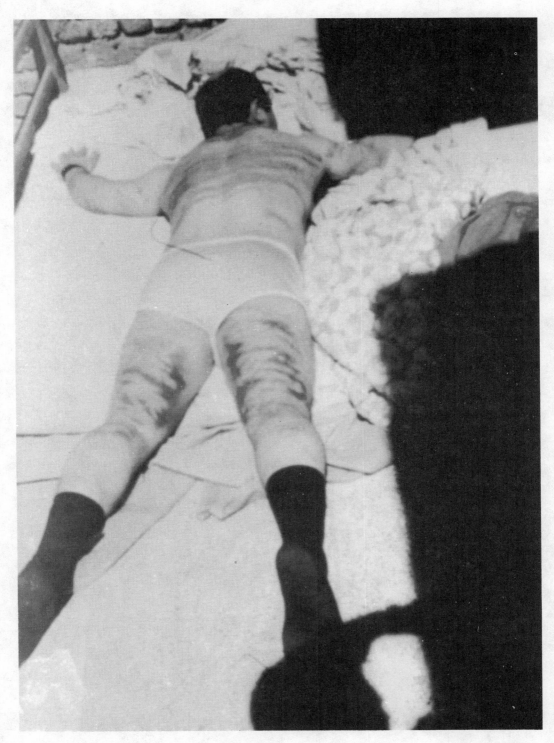

Flogging is used as a judicial punishment for a wide variety of offences. This man was flogged, in 1988, for shouting slogans against the war with Iraq. Amnesty International believes that tens of thousands of floggings have been carried out since the 1979 revolution.

CHAPTER THREE: POLITICAL IMPRISONMENT

In 1987 thousands of political prisoners were being held in Iran, including many hundreds of prisoners of conscience. Many of these political prisoners had been detained in the early 1980s. Some were supporters of opposition groups which had resorted to armed opposition against the government, such as the PMOI, the KDPI, Komala and various factions of the PFOI. A large proportion of the alleged supporters of these groups who remained in prison had not themselves been involved in violent political activities. Those arrested by the authorities for taking part in armed activities were executed in their thousands in 1980 and 1981, while others were killed in armed clashes.

As the clerical leadership tightened its grip on power, and in the context of the war with neighbouring Iraq, all forms of political activity, outside the closed circle of the religious leadership, were suppressed.

None of these thousands of political prisoners was given a fair trial in accordance with international standards. Some were held in indefinite pre-trial detention. Others were tortured and forced to confess to offences which then formed the basis for their conviction after summary trials before Islamic Revolutionary Courts. Many of those imprisoned were very young at the time of their detention; young people in their teens and early twenties who had been caught up in the excitement and political turmoil of the post-revolutionary period.

In February 1988 Davoud Karimi, a senior official in the Islamic Revolutionary Committee, announced that there were approximately 9,000 supporters of illegal opposition groups in prison in Iran. In May 1988 the arrests of 200 supporters of the PFOI (majority) and of the Tudeh Party were announced in Mashhad. Following the armed incursion into western Iran by a PMOI-led force in July 1988, dozens of former political prisoners, held for short periods during the early 1980s for alleged association with the PMOI, were rearrested. In the Iranian year ending 20 March 1989, 1,273 people were said to have been arrested for affiliation to opposition groups, according to a statement by another Islamic Revolutionary Committee official (Iran Yearbook 1989/90).

It is difficult to quantify the number of political prisoners, as many political arrests are believed to have taken place in secret. However, in June 1990 it appeared that there were substantially fewer political prisoners than in 1987. One obvious reason for this was the mass execution of political prisoners which took place between July 1988 and January 1989 (see Chapter Two). Many prisoners have been forced to remain in prison after the expiry of their sentences, subjected to arbitrary imprisonment with no judicial sanction. However, large numbers of political prisoners have also benefited from general prisoner amnesties.

3.1 Agencies Which Carry Out Political Arrests

There are three law enforcement agencies under the jurisdiction of the Minister of the Interior: the Gendarmerie, the Police and the Islamic Revolutionary Committees. Of these, the Committees are most centrally involved in the cases of political prisoners.

The Committees are an armed force which grew out of popular neighbourhood groups formed during the revolution. They have primary responsibility for policing activities in the fields of drug-trafficking, anti-Islamic and sacreligious acts, and illegal activities by opposition groups. There is a good deal of overlap between their work and that of the police, who are responsible for criminal investigations.

The Islamic Revolutionary Guards Corps (IRGC), an autonomous branch of the armed forces, also has its origins in the popular committees of the revolutionary period. It has responsibility for combatting plots of internal enemies which has led to its involvement in political detentions.

In June 1990 the Islamic Consultative Assembly passed articles of a law merging the Gendarmerie, the Police and the Islamic Revolutionary Committees into a single organization to be known as the Islamic Revolution Security Guard. The merger is to take place within one year of the law being enacted.

3.2 Prisoner Amnesties

Prisoners in Iran, including prisoners of conscience and other political prisoners, have periodically benefited from amnesties. Those involving the greatest number of prisoners have been granted to mark the anniversaries of the foundation of the Islamic Republic in February 1979. On the 10th anniversary the authorities announced that 2,600 out of 3,500 political prisoners who they acknowledged were then held in Iran were to be released on the recommendation of the Minister of Intelligence, Mohammad Reyshahri. He is reported to have said:

> "The information system within the Islamic system does not exclude legitimate rights. Therefore, following an arrest, if it is felt that the offender has been corrected or that his release is not dangerous to the security of the country, we make a suggestion regarding his release even if he is given a long sentence or even death." (BBC Summary of World Broadcasts, 16 February 1989)

The role played by the Ministry of Intelligence, which has no judicial authority under the Constitution of the Islamic Republic, in determining which political prisoners should be executed during the latter part of 1988 was described in Chapter Two. The Ministry's involvement in decisions about which political prisoners should be amnestied also suggests that areas of decision making which should properly be the province of the judiciary are in fact under the control of the executive political authority of the Ministry of Intelligence. This influence has worked to the detriment of the independence of the judiciary and has deprived political prisoners of judicial safeguards.

The February 1990 prisoner amnesty to mark the anniversary of the foundation of the Islamic Republic differed from that of the previous year in that the beneficiaries were apparently selected by a judicial authority, Ayatollah Yazdi, the Head of the Judiciary. Political prisoners were reportedly not included in the 1990 amnesty. However, it may be a positive development that the judiciary has gained influence in this area of decision making. It may also be significant that the former Minister of Intelligence , Mohammad Reyshahri, was appointed to a senior post in the judiciary, that of Prosecutor General, in July 1989.

A further cause for concern about amnesties for political prisoners is that they appear to have been dependent on prisoners renouncing their former political ideas -- even to the extent of making videotaped confessions of their "crimes" for possible broadcast on Iranian television. For example, it has been alleged that some women prisoners of conscience in Evin Prison have been offered an amnesty if they agree to condemn publicly the political activities of their husbands, who were executed in 1988. These attempts to force prisoners to change their political opinions are in contravention of Article 19 of the ICCPR, which states: "Everyone shall have the right to hold opinions without interference." It is also clear that the system of granting periodic amnesties to political prisoners is no alternative to a fair trial in accordance with international standards, and to an independent judiciary.

3.3 Political Arrests

Article 32 of the Constitution of the Islamic Republic of Iran is specific about procedures which must be followed in order to carry out an arrest:

> "No one can be arrested except in accordance with judgment and the procedure established by law. In the case of arrest, charges and supporting evidence must be communicated immediately in writing to the prisoner and be elucidated to him..."

Speaking to the Special Representative of the UN Human Rights Commission during his visit to Tehran in January 1990, the Deputy Minister of the Interior is reported to have said:

> "Warrants are required for all arrests except in cases of flagrante delicto. The time limit for the preliminary investigation is 24 hours, after which the case is transferred to the competent judge or the detainee is released." (para 123 op.cit.)

In practice, political arrests are carried out in an arbitrary manner by the Islamic Revolutionary Committees and by the IRGC. One example was the arrest of Mohammad Tavassoli-Hojati at his home on 31 May 1988. He was a member of the Executive Committee of the Association for the Defence of Freedom and Sovereignty of the Iranian Nation (ADFSIN), an organization associated with the Islamic Republic's first Prime Minister, Dr Mehdi Bazargan. The UN Special Representative, who spoke with Mohammad Tavassoli-Hojati in Tehran in January 1990, described the arrest:

> "A group of armed persons broke into his house and took all his personal belongings, and brought him to Touhid Prison where he was interrogated for five and a half months by agents of the Ministry of Information. He was not informed of the charges against him, and was not presented to a court within 24 hours. ...After five and a half months he was transferred to Evin Prison where he had to remain for another three months. Finally he received a list of charges as follows: activities against the security of the government, activities to topple the government and assistance to the enemy. A meeting Prime Minister Bazargan had with the United States Ambassador in 1979 with the express agreement of Ayatollah Khomeini was cited as proof for these charges. He was held for eight and a half months in solitary confinement...."(op.cit. para 208)

Mohammad Tavassoli-Hojati was arrested together with other members of the Executive Committee of ADFSIN: Dr Ali Ardalan, Hossein Shah-Hosseini, Khosro Mansourian, Hashem Sabbaghian and Ahmad Zanjani. They were never brought to trial. Amnesty International believes that they were prisoners of conscience, detained for their non-violent political activity. The reason for their imprisonment appears to have been their support for an open letter from Dr Bazargan to Ayatollah Khomeini calling for a ceasefire in the Gulf War. They were all eventually released, the last of them in February 1989, over six months after Iran had accepted the terms of a ceasefire.

In June 1990 some of the signatories to an open letter addressed to President Rafsanjani, including Mohammad Tavassoli-Hojati, were arrested. The letter, signed by 90 people, criticized the lack of implementation of rights and freedoms guaranteed by the Constitution of the Islamic Republic of Iran, as well as the government's economic and foreign policies. Some of those detained were also members of ADFSIN, or of the Freedom Movement of Iran, and were associated with Dr Bazargan, who is Secretary-General of the Freedom Movement of Iran and President of ADFSIN. The exact number of those arrested is not known, but by July 1990 Amnesty International had obtained the names of more than 20 people, some of whom were elderly and in poor health.

The declaration of establishment of ADFSIN, promulgated in March 1986, makes clear its commitment to operate as an "open and legal association". It had applied for registration under the Political Parties Act of 1981, but had received no decision. The UN Special Representative reported that, during his visit to Iran in January 1990, an Interior Ministry official told him that although ADFSIN did not have legal authorization, "they criticize the Government and no one interferes with them." (UN document

E/CN.4/1990/24). However, on 14 June 1990, after the arrests of ADFSIN members had already started, the government ordered the dissolution of the association. Among the aims described in ADFSIN's charter are:

"To endeavour to provide legal protection and safeguard of the people's rights, men or women, and legal security for all in full equality before the law." (Article 5)

"To endeavour towards the realization of the principle of the innocence of the accused, open and equal treatment before the law, the right to legal representation, trial by jury of political and press offences, and prevention of illegal trials and punishments."(Article 8)

Amnesty International considered all those detained in connection with the open letter to be prisoners of conscience and launched a campaign for their immediate and unconditional release. The prisoners included Ali Ardalan, the 73-year-old Head of ADFSIN's Executive Committee. A former finance minister in Mehdi Bazargan's government, he was previously arrested in September 1981, released four years later and rearrested in May 1988, when he was held for several months. His most recent arrest took place at his home in Tehran on 19 June 1990, when he was allegedly beaten. Ali Ardalan was known to suffer from heart disease, and his incommunicado detention and reported beating gave particular cause for concern.

Other former ministers imprisoned in connection with the open letter included Hossein Bani Assadi, former deputy prime minister, Hashem Sabbaghian, former minister of the interior, Reza Sadr, former minister of trade, Ezzatollah Sahabi, former minister of budget and planning and Hossein Shah-Hosseini, another former deputy prime minister. A number of other prominent figures associated with Dr Bazargan were also among those imprisoned. All the prisoners were reportedly held in Evin Prison in Tehran and put under pressure to make televised "confessions".

The experiences of the supporters of Dr Bazargan, who have been practically alone during the last three years in attempting to function as a political opposition within the law inside Iran, show the intolerance of the government towards political dissent and its willingness to use imprisonment to silence its critics. Some have a long history of persecution for their political activities dating back to the time of the Shah.

The continuing suppression of the peaceful political activity of Dr Bazargan and his supporters gives the lie to such statements as that made by the then Minister of Intelligence, Mohammad Reyshahri, on 14 February 1989:

"I say decisively here and now that not a single individual has been arrested in this country for his views, nor will there ever be such arrests." (BBC Summary of World Broadcasts, 14 February 1989)

In practice, freedom of political activity has been circumscribed by the widespread imprisonment of prisoners of conscience.

Thousands of people have been subjected to arbitrary arrest and held indefinitely without charge or trial. One woman told Amnesty International about the arrest of her cousin, Reza, in a village near Shiraz. Reza had been imprisoned briefly in 1981 because he was suspected of involvement with the PMOI, but he was released and had not been involved in politics since then. In August 1988 four or five armed men in uniform came to the family home one evening. They said they wanted to ask Reza some questions and they took him away. The armed men instructed his parents to go to the IRGC headquarters in Shiraz the next morning to obtain information about their son. However, when they went there they were told "your son is a hypocrite", and that it was necessary to make inquiries about him. The parents were not permitted to see him and were not informated of his whereabouts. Five months after his arrest, his family had received not further news about him.

Even when prisoners are tried and sentenced, they often remain in detention long after the sentence has expired. One woman supporter of the left-wing opposition group Rah-e Kargar, was detained while travelling in Iranian Kurdistan in 1982. She was held for over 15 months before being tried before a Revolutionary Court in Evin Prison, Tehran. The hearing lasted a matter of seconds -- she was not even allowed to sit down as the religious judge told her they would have to wash the chair afterwards if she did. Three months later she found out she had been sentenced to two years' imprisonment. However, she was not released when the two years expired and her imprisonment only ended when she escaped from another prison in November 1988.

In some cases, relatives of people being sought by the authorities are reported to have been imprisoned either as a substitute or as a form of hostage, to put pressure on the wanted person to give him or herself up. In one case, in October 1989, an Iranian political refugee living in Europe contacted Amnesty International to report that his mother had been detained in Qasr Prison in Tehran when the authorities learned that he had left the country illegally. He asked that no publicity should be given to the case for fear of worsening the situation of his relatives in Iran. Other refugees reporting arrests and detentions of people in Iran have expressed similar apprehension.

Suspicion of involvement in illegal political activity, or association with someone suspected of being so involved, remains sufficient to warrant unlimited detention without charge or trial. This is in contravention of the Iranian Constitution and of international human rights standards to which Iran is committed. For example, Article 9(2) of the ICCPR prohibits arbitrary arrest and requires that:

> "Anyone who is arrested shall be informed, at the time of arrest, of the reasons for his arrest and shall be promptly informed of any charges against him."

It also requires under Article 9(4) that:

"Anyone who is deprived of his liberty by arrest or detention shall be entitled to take proceedings before a court, in order that that court may decide without delay on the lawfulness of his detention and order his release if the detention is not lawful."

The Body of Principles for the Protection of All Persons Under Any Form of Detention or Imprisonment, adopted by the UN General Assembly on 9 December 1988 by consensus, which is applicable to all states, requires under Principle 10:

"Anyone who is arrested shall be informed at the time of his arrest of the reason for his arrest and shall be promptly informed of any charges against him."

Principle 1(1) requires that:

"A person shall not be kept in detention without being given an effective opportunity to be heard promptly by a judicial or other authority."

Arbitrary detention procedures leave open the possibility that people may be detained as a consequence of mistaken identity. It also allows those in authority to imprison people against whom they have a personal grudge. Amnesty International has received reports of people being imprisoned because of personal disputes or family quarrels with officials in the Islamic Revolutionary Committees. A system which strips the individual of even the most basic safeguards against arbitrary arrest and detention leaves itself open to such abuse.

3.4 Long-Term Political Prisoners

Victims of arbitrary arrest, including many prisoners of conscience, remain in prison years after their arrest. Some have been sentenced to long prison terms after unfair trials by revolutionary courts; some are simply held indefinitely without charge or trial, or after their sentences have expired.

It has often been difficult to obtain information about political prisoners in Iran. The authorities have not responded to inquiries about the reasons for arrest, or the trial procedures followed, in particular cases. For example, Amnesty International wrote to the Iranian authorities in April 1990 to seek information about the reasons for the arrest of 65 people at a political demonstration reportedly held at Mellat Park in north Tehran on 15 April 1990. To date, it has received no reply to this inquiry or to similar inquiries about other reported arrests at political demonstrations in the early part of 1990.

Relatives of prisoners have been unwilling to disclose publicly their concern about family members in prison for fear of reprisals by the authorities. Similarly, it has often been necessary for Amnesty International to describe its concerns about the treatment of political prisoners in Iran in general terms, without naming individuals even when they are known. As a result, many thousands of political prisoners have gone to their deaths anonymously, or are known simply as names on a list. Hundreds of other prisoners are incarcerated in similar circumstances.

However, a few prisoners are already so well known that reference to their plight cannot place them in greater jeopardy. Their cases are no more than illustrative of many others in which men and women have been imprisoned in Iran on account of their political beliefs and activities.

Among those currently held in Evin Prison are women prisoners such as Mariam Firouz and Malakeh Mohammadi, detained since the dissolution of the Tudeh Party in 1983. They were prominent in the leadership of the organization, which was legal at the time of their arrest.

In early 1983 the Tudeh Party's organizational structures were dismantled, its premises closed, and its newspapers and publications proscribed. By mid-1983 the leadership of the party along with hundreds of its supporters had been imprisoned. On 14 May 1983, the Prosecutor General of the Islamic Revolutionary Court announced that "1,500 members of the defunct Tudeh Party" had been arrested throughout the country. Many were tortured to force them to confess to crimes such as treason or espionage on behalf of the Soviet Union. Some were forced to make televised confessions. Prisoners who had confessed were then brought before Islamic Revolutionary Courts where they were given summary trials (see Chapter Two).

Similar methods were employed by the authorities to clamp down on the activities of a variety of political movements which had sprung up in the unprecedented freedom of the post-revolutionary period. In 1981, thousands of men and women, mostly young, were killed and thousands more detained when the confrontation between the government and the PMOI was at its height. This confrontation led to armed attacks on members of the government and pitched battles in the streets of Tehran and other cities.

Thousands of prisoners were executed after summary trials: over 2,400 recorded by Amnesty International in the first six months of 1981 alone. Thousands more remained in prison, including an unknown number of prisoners of conscience: sympathizers of the PMOI who had neither used nor advocated violence; and supporters of a wide variety of non-violent political organizations such as the National Democratic Front, Rah-e Kargar and certain monarchist organizations. Many of these prisoners died in the massacre of 1988, after years of unjust imprisonment. Some of those who survived remain in prison to this day.

Amnesty International is concerned that all prisoners of conscience

should be released unconditionally. The organization believes that there
is an urgent need for the detention of all political prisoners to be
reviewed by an independent judicial authority empowered to order the
immediate release of those against whom there is no evidence of their
having committed any recognizably criminal offence. Where such a review
concludes that there is a case to be answered by the prisoner, a fair trial
in accordance with international standards should be held. Such a process
would contribute to the release of the many men and women imprisoned in
Iran solely for their non-violent political activities.

CHAPTER FOUR: TORTURE

In its 1987 report Amnesty International noted reports of torture and
ill-treatment of prisoners in Iran and proposed measures that the Iranian
authorities should take to safeguard prisoners from such abuse. Three
years later, none of these measures is known to have been taken by the
Iranian Government and prisoners continue to be subject to torture and ill-
treatment.

Torture is used to extract confessions from prisoners held in pre-
trial incommunicado detention. It is also used to extract information such
as the names of supporters of opposition political groups, or the
whereabouts of individuals wanted by the authorities. Torture for the
purpose of extracting confessions is explicitly forbidden by the
Constitution of the Islamic Republic of Iran (Article 38), but this is a
prohibition which has been routinely flouted.

4.1   Torture and Cruel, Inhuman or Degrading Treatment

Torture, beating and intimidation of prisoners is reportedly widespread
both during pre-trial detention and following trial and sentence. Such
abuses appear to be condoned by the authorities: despite hundreds of
torture allegations made by former prisoners since 1979, many of them
substantiated by medical evidence, Amnesty International knows of none that
has been investigated since an inconclusive inquiry into torture in 1980 to
1981. Amnesty International is also not aware of any member of the
security forces having been brought to justice for torturing or ill-
treating prisoners.

The type of torture most frequently reported to Amnesty International
is flogging with whips or cables. Prisoners are whipped on the feet or on
the back while tied face downwards on a bed frame. Suspension by the
wrists is also common, often with one arm forced behind the back and the
other over the shoulder so that the wrists meet behind the back, a position
which causes intense pain. Psychological torture, including mock
execution, is also reported.

Prisoners may be held in indefinite incommunicado detention with no
means of challenging their imprisonment before a court (see Chapter Three)
or of seeking redress for ill-treatment and torture suffered while in the
hands of the detaining authorities. Amnesty International knows of no
system of prison inspection in Iran, such as exists in many countries,
which could monitor prisoners' treatment, record and investigate their
complaints, and help them seek redress. The circumstances in which torture
occurs in Iran are illustrated by the following case histories. (Note:
names marked with an asterisk have been altered to protect their relatives
remaining in Iran.)

Dr Ahmed Danesh

Dr. Ahmed Danesh, a surgeon, was executed during the mass killing of political prisoners in 1988. He had been imprisoned since 1983 because of his support for the Tudeh Party. In May 1987 he had written a letter from Evin Prison to Ayatollah Montazeri, at that time the designated successor to Ayatollah Khomeini as Leader of the Islamic Republic. A copy of the letter reached Amnesty International after his death. In it he wrote that the laws of Islam and the land, and the stated policy of the leadership, were not being followed in Evin Prison:

> "Even though torture is forbidden by our constitution, I have been tortured and have repeatedly witnessed others being beaten unmercifully. I have heard with my own ears how people crawled along the floor because they were unable to move in any other way after they had been tortured. I have seen people vomiting as a result of the unbearable pain and wounds inflicted by torture. They lost so much body fluid that their skins dried out and they could have died at any moment. I have seen people whose urine consisted mainly of blood and who had to be put on kidney machines because of kidney failure as a result of beatings.

> "Despite everything laid down in the constitution and the law I have seen prisoners made fun of and beaten simply for mentioning their rights under these instruments."

Fathi*

Fathi was 22 years old when he was arrested by armed men and taken to a prison run by the Ministry of Intelligence in Zahedan. This was a secret detention centre, according to Fathi, its location is not even known to local people. In a letter to Amnesty International written after he had escaped from Iran to seek asylum abroad, Fathi described his imprisonment in Zahedan in 1988:

> "When I arrived at the detention centre I was strapped to a bed face down and beaten with whips and cables while they asked questions about my alleged political activities for Peykar [an illegal left-wing political organization].

> "The interrogators threatened to kill me and dump my body in the desert. On one occasion an interrogator held a pistol to my neck while another guard fired his pistol into the air. It was an absolutely terrifying experience."

Fathi was released in February 1989. He had not been charged or tried. His back still carries scars from the beatings he was given and he has a number of other scars caused by cigarette burns inflicted while he was in detention.

Mohammad Tavassoli-Hojati

Mohammad Tavassoli-Hojati, a former mayor of Tehran and a leading member of Dr Mehdi Bazargan's Freedom Movement, was arrested on 31 May 1988 (see Chapter Three above). The UN Special Representative, who interviewed Mohammad Tavassoli-Hojati during his visit to Iran in January 1990, recorded the following:

> "His interrogators were trying by every means
> including beatings, insults and threats to make him
> confess that he had passed information to the enemy....
> He was held for eight and a half months in solitary
> confinement."
> (Paragraph 208, UN Special Representative's
> Report)

Mohammad Tavassoli-Hojati was given a list of charges some months after his arrest, but he was never brought to trial.

Reza*

Reza was interviewed by Amnesty International in Europe where he is now seeking political asylum. He was arrested from his home by armed officers from the Islamic Revolutionary Committee in March 1989.

> "I was taken to Qasr Prison in Tehran and put in a small
> room like a cupboard. It had no window and was only about one
> metre long by 75 centimetres across, so I was unable to lie down
> and had to sleep in a sitting position.
>
> "Every other day I was taken to another room and questioned.
> While being questioned I was beaten with fists and rifle butts.
> Each interrogation session lasted approximately 45 minutes to an
> hour."

Reza was never charged with any specific offence, rather he was interrogated about his political views. His interrogators wanted him to admit that he and his family had monarchist sympathies. He says he confessed what they asked him to, partly because of the beating, and partly because the authorities already knew about the monarchist sympathies of his family.

"After about seven or eight days in detention I started to vomit blood. In a state of near unconsciousness I was allowed to see a doctor in the prison. He diagnosed that I had a stomach ulcer. I was then returned to my cell.

"For the next few days I was not treated harshly by my interrogators. However, about two weeks after my arrest some prison guards came to my cell at four or five in the morning. 'Come along, you're finished,' they said to me. They blindfolded me, tied my hands behind my back, and took me to the prison yard. There they made me stand against a wall -- I could hear there were a number of other prisoners next to me. I was asked if I had anything to say as a last statement. I said nothing. Then I heard the order to shoot being given."

Reza was not hit by any of the bullets. He was untied, and as he was being taken back to his cell he lifted his blindfold and saw that eight prisoners had been executed and three, including him, were being led away.

After this, questioning continued. He was kept in his solitary cell at first, then moved to another part of Qasr Prison where serious criminal offenders were held. He was kept there for about six weeks and taken out for interrogation three times. He was again beaten by his interrogators on the first two occasions, but during his last interrogation session, the day before his release, he was not roughly treated.

He was released from prison after six weeks on payment of a financial surety by his family. About one month after his release he left Iran on a false passport.

This was not Reza's first experience of torture at the hands of the security forces.

"In the summer of 1987 I went with a girl from Tehran to visit my aunt in the north of the country near the Caspian Sea. We were travelling by car and at 11pm were stopped by Islamic Revolutionary Committee personnel in Ramsar. They asked us to show our identity papers. These showed that we were not married, or related in any way, and the Committee officers accused us of involvement in immoral acts. I was separated from the girl at the Committee headquarters. They tied me up with one arm twisted behind my back and the other arm across my chest. I was then suspended by my wrists from a tree in the courtyard and left hanging for about five hours."

He was held in Ramsar for two days. At his trial, during which he was not allowed to speak, he was sentenced to two months' imprisonment and 200 lashes. His family were allowed to pay a large sum of money to reduce the number of lashes to 100. These were administered in the public square in front of the town hall in Ramsar.

Badri*

Badri spoke to Amnesty International in Europe, where she now lives. Her husband had been detained and executed in 1981, apparently because of his employment by SAVAK, the secret police of the Shah's administration prior to the revolution. She had been arrested briefly in 1981. Her second and most recent arrest took place in February 1989. Four armed men from the Islamic Revolutionary Committee came to her home in Tehran during the afternoon. They were looking for her husband's brother, but he had been warned that the authorities were looking for him so he was not there.

> "I was blindfolded and taken to a prison in Tehran which I knew to be Qasr Prison. There I was put into a single cell measuring about three by four metres containing a bed, a sink and a toilet. I was held in solitary confinement in this cell for 25 days and not permitted to see anyone except the interrogators.

> "Every day I was interrogated by between three and five guards who beat me with their hands, with rifle butts and with whips. Sometimes I would lose consciousness, but they revived me by throwing cold water over me.

> "As well as the beatings, they pulled out a number of my teeth. This was done, without any anaesthetic, by prison guards wearing Committee uniforms."

Her interrogators wanted to find out where her brother-in-law was hiding. Badri broke down under torture and told them. She was later informed that he had been arrested. Once the interrogators had obtained the information they wanted, Badri was released. As she no longer felt safe in Iran she paid a bribe to obtain a passport and left the country. In Europe she was examined by a doctor and a dentist. They concluded in their report that "the objective findings are consistent with the described torture".

Ayatollah Yazdi, the Head of the Judiciary, is reported to have said on 20 March 1990 that "the issues of justice, health, clothing and living conditions of prisoners are being given greater attention". Amnesty International considers that high priority must also be given to bringing an end to widespread, institutionalized torture. Amnesty International's recommendations from its 1987 report, on which the government has failed to act, remain directly relevant as positive steps towards this aim.

4.1.1 Amnesty International's Recommendations

Amnesty International recognizes that torture is forbidden in the Constitution of the Islamic Republic of Iran "for the purpose of extracting confessions or gaining information" and that the infliction or ordering of ill-treatment of prisoners is a punishable offence under Iranian law. Nevertheless, Amnesty International considers that further measures are urgently needed to ensure that torture and ill-treatment of prisoners does not occur. Such measures should, in general, include the following recommendations included in Amnesty International's 1987 report:

"(a) clear and publicized condemnation of the use of torture should be made by the highest authorities in the land;

(b) all detainees should be held in publicly recognized places of detention or prisons, and not in secret places;

(c) legislation prohibiting torture should be strengthened to include an unequivocal prohibition of torture in the Constitution and should be seen to be carried out;

(d) those responsible for inflicting or ordering the use of torture should be brought to justice;

(e) the training of all law enforcement agencies should emphasize the total prohibition of the use of torture;

(f) victims of torture should be compensated.

"Amnesty International is concerned about the lack of basic safeguards in the treatment of political detainees. It respectfully recommends that the following steps be taken without delay:

(a) a legal limit should be prescribed and strictly enforced to restrict incommunicado detention; in Amnesty International's experience, prolonged incommunicado detention is frequently conducive to torture and ill-treatment;

(b) anyone arrested or detained should have the right to challenge his or her detention before a judicial authority, in accordance with Article 9 (3) of the International Covenant on Civil and Political Rights. In the opinion of the Human Rights Committee the delay between arrest and such procedure "must not exceed a few days" (General Comment 8 (16));

(c)   there should be a set limit to solitary confinement, which the
       the Human Rights Committee has held "may, according to the
       circumstances, and especially when the person is kept
       incommunicado, be contrary to... [Article 7 of the International
       Covenant on Civil and Political Rights]" which forbids the use of
       torture (General Comment 7 (16));

(d)   that, in addition to being permitted family visits, as mentioned
       above, all detainees should be granted, in all cases, prompt and
       regular access to legal counsel of their own choosing, as well
       as to qualified medical personnel when necessary.

   "Amnesty International knows of numerous allegations of torture and
ill-treatment, both physical and psychological, of prisoners in the Islamic
Republic of Iran. The organization respectfully urges that a public and
impartial investigation be conducted into allegations of torture and ill-
treatment, and that there should be a thorough review of the administrative
and judicial procedures regulating the arrest, confinement and
interrogation of political suspects. The inquiry's findings and its
working methods should be made public.

   "Pending the establishment of such a commission, its findings and
recommendations, Amnesty International recommends the immediate
establishment of basic, practical safeguards. These should include:

(a)   clear notification to the next of kin that someone has been
       arrested and clear indication of his or her whereabouts;

(b)   access for each detainee to relatives and a lawyer of his or her
       own choosing, both immediately after arrest and at brief,
       regular intervals thereafter;

(c)   each detainee should be examined by a qualified doctor on arrival
       in prison and periodically thereafter; a copy of the medical
       report (fully respecting the confidentiality of its contents)
       should be kept by a central authority;

(d)   frequent and unannounced visits should be made by people
       independent of the authorities responsible for detaining,
       investigating or prosecuting the prisoners. The purpose of this
       should be to inspect all prisons and detention centres, to record
       and seek redress for prisoners' complaints and to monitor
       standards of medical treatment, food and hygiene.

   "On 10 December 1984 the United Nations General Assembly adopted the
Convention against Torture and Other Cruel, Inhuman or Degrading Treatment
or Punishment, through Resolution 39/46, which called upon "...all
Governments to consider signing and ratifying the Convention as a matter of
priority." The Convention obliges all States Parties to it to make torture
a punishable offence and to prevent the use of torture in their

jurisdictions. Amnesty International respectfully urges the Government of the Islamic Republic of Iran to take immediate steps to become a party to the Convention against Torture."

4.2 Recommendations of the UN Special Rapporteur on Torture

The necessity of these recommendations is further emphasized by the recent recommendations of the UN Special Rapporteur on torture in his 18 December 1989 report:

> "(a) Since a great number of the allegations received by the Special Rapporteur referred to torture practised during incommunicado detention, incommunicado detention should be prohibited;
>
> (b) Other allegations referred to torture practised during illegal detention before a detainee was presented to a judge. Those who act contrary to the rules prescribed for a lawful arrest should be subjected to appropriate sanctions;
>
> (c) Any person who is arrested should be given access to legal counsel no later than 24 hours after his arrest; his relatives should be informed promptly of his arrest and the place where he is detained;
>
> (d) Any person who is arrested should be medically examined immediately after his arrest. Such examination should take place regularly, and in any case should be compulsory whenever the detainee is transferred to another place of detention;
>
> (e) All interrogation sessions should be recorded; the identity of all persons present should be included in the records. Evidence obtained from the detainee during non-recorded interrogations should not be admitted in court;
>
> (f) All places of detention should be regularly inspected by independent inspection teams. Such teams should be allowed to speak with detainees in private;
>
> (g) In every case of death of a person during his detention or shortly after his release, an inquiry into the cause of death and the circumstances surrounding it should be held by a judicial or other impartial authority;
>
> (h) Everyone should be entitled to file a complaint about torture or severe maltreatment with an independent authority; the official in charge of the investigation of the detainee's case cannot be considered to be an independent authority;
>
> (i) Whenever a person is found to be responsible for acts of torture or severe maltreatment he should be brought to trial; if

found guilty, he should be severely punished;

(j) The Body of Principles for the Protection of All Persons under Any Form of Detention or Imprisonment, the Code of Conduct for Law Enforcement Officials and the Standard Minimum Rules for the Treatment of Prisoners should be translated into national languages and used as teaching material during training courses for law enforcement personnel and members of the security forces entrusted with the task of protecting internal law and order. In particular, such personnel should be instructed on their duty to disobey orders received from a superior to practise torture."

4.3 Punishments which Constitute Torture or Cruel, Inhuman or Degrading Punishment

The Islamic Penal Code of Iran provides for the punishment of amputation of limbs or fingers for theft, and of flogging for a wide range of offences.

Flogging is very widely applied as a punishment in Iran, even for relatively minor offences. The extent to which flogging is applied as a judicial punishment can be seen from the official figure of 4,467 as the number of acts of corporal punishment carried out in the Tehran district alone in the Iranian calendar year 1365 (March 1986 to March 1987). (Jomhouriy-e Eslami newspaper, 17 March 1987) Amnesty International believes that the majority of these acts of corporal punishment were floggings, although the figure also seems to include an unspecified number of amputations.

Amnesty International has not been able to obtain official statistics showing the full extent of the application of corporal punishment. However, extrapolating from the official figure quoted above, it seems reasonable to suppose that perhaps tens of thousands of judicially authorized floggings take place in Iran each year.

Amnesty International's 1987 report noted the organization's concern about "reports of the summary nature of criminal trial proceedings in such cases". This concern has been heightened by the judiciary's measures to speed up the punishment of offenders (see Chapter Two), which have eroded yet further safeguards against miscarriages of justice taking place.

The Penal Code gives some indication of how the punishment of flogging should be inflicted. According to Article 115, the punishment for fornication is prescribed thus:

"A man, while standing and his body naked except for a cover of his private parts, is whipped all over the body except on his head, face and private parts. A woman, however, is whipped while sitting with her dress tied to her body."

The Penal Code also stipulates that the flogging for certain offences can be carried out while a man is fully clothed, and with less force than in the punishment for fornication.

Amputation has been used as a punishment for theft. Article 218 of the Penal Code stipulates:

> "<u>Hadd</u> for theft for the first time is the dismembering of four fingers of the right hand of the thief from the fingers' extremity so that only the thumb and palm of the thief remain..."

During 1989 Amnesty International recorded nine cases of amputation for theft, although the organization does not have a complete record of all such punishments.

Sentences of flogging may be imposed by both Penal Courts, and by Islamic Revolutionary Courts. Amputations appear to have been used as punishment for repeated theft, which comes under the jurisdiction of Penal Court (One).

Amputations are reportedly sometimes carried out using an electric guillotine, and it appears that medical supervision is usual. For example, on 18 January 1990 a convicted thief had four fingers of his right hand amputated in Tehran, after being sentenced by a court in Shahroud. The amputation had to be postponed once because the convict was found to be suffering from high blood pressure.

4.3.1 Amnesty International's Recommendations

Amputation and flogging are forms of torture or cruel, inhuman or degrading punishment prohibited by international law and, as such, should be replaced with penalties which are compatible with international human rights standards. In its General Comment 7(16) the Human Rights Committee provided an authoritative interpretation of Article 7 of the ICCPR, which prohibits torture or cruel, inhuman and degrading treatment or punishment. It states:

> "As appears from the terms of this article, the scope of protection goes far beyond torture as normally understood. It may not be necessary to draw sharp distinctions between the various prohibited forms of treatment or punishment. The distinctions depend on the kind, purpose and severity of the particular treatment. In the view of the Committee the prohibition must extend to corporal punishment, including excessive chastisement as an educational or disciplinary measure..." (UN document A/37/40, at 94-95 (1985))

As for amputation, in August 1984 the UN Sub-Commission on Prevention of Discrimination and Protection of Minorities adopted a resolution

(1984/22) recommending the UN Commission on Human Rights to urge governments which had legislation providing for the penalty of amputation to prescribe different punishments in accordance with Article 5 of the Universal Declaration of Human Rights, which prohibits "cruel, inhuman or degrading treatment or punishment."

Amnesty International recommends the replacement of such punishments by other penalties which are consistent with recognized international standards for the prevention and punishment of crime and the treatment of offenders.

CHAPTER FIVE:

THE IRANIAN GOVERNMENT'S RESPONSE TO CRITICISM OF ITS HUMAN RIGHTS RECORD

In January 1990, after five years of refusing access, the Iranian Government finally agreed to allow the Special Representative of the UN Human Rights Commission to visit the country to conduct inquiries into the human rights situation.

Amnesty International welcomes the Iranian Government's willingness to cooperate with the Commission on Human Rights. It hopes that this cooperation will continue, and will result in the speedy implementation of effective safeguards to ensure that the provisions of the international human rights covenants promoted by the Commission are enjoyed by Iranian citizens.

At the same time Amnesty International is aware that in recent years the Iranian Government has conducted an increasingly vociferous publicity campaign at the UN and in other international forums where human rights are discussed, defending its record on human rights and attacking its critics.

Two dominant themes emerge from the Iranian Government's responses to criticism of its human rights record. The first is an assertion that a legal system based on the divinely ordained precepts of Islamic Law is not subject to the provisions of international human rights standards. The second is an objection to the international community expressing concern about human rights violations suffered by members and supporters of armed opposition groups while not showing an equal concern for the victims of political violence or terrorism.

It is the second of these themes, relating to the activities of armed opposition groups, to which the Iranian Government has resorted most frequently in its public responses to criticism of its human rights record. Vigorous condemnation of the activities of armed opposition groups is a policy on which all factions within the clerical leadership appear able to agree. Reference to the acute circumstances of internal armed conflict and the criminal behaviour of non-governmental groups is widely employed by governments seeking to justify their actions in response to allegations of human rights violations.

On the other hand, the question of the applicability of international human rights standards to countries seeking to implement a system of Islamic Law appears to be a subject on which there are differing views within the clerical leadership. It is also the case that there is a broad international consensus recognizing the universality of human rights standards set down in the Universal Declaration of Human Rights and the primary covenants. As the Special Representative of the UN Human Rights Commission observed when discussing this issue in his most recent report:

> "The international system for the protection of human
> rights does not permit any exception based on internal
> legal systems; it is for each State to conform to
> International Law." (UN document E/CN.4/1990/24, para. 75)

5.1 Islam and International Law

One of the basic principles of Amnesty International's work is its
impartiality, which it puts into practice by applying the same standards to
all governments and to all country situations. The organization bases its
work on the provisions of international human rights treaties. These
treaties, such as the ICCPR, are commitments entered into freely by
governments. Amnesty International seeks to ensure that governments fulfil
their obligations as State Parties to these treaties in those areas which
are of concern to the organization: the immediate release of all prisoners
of conscience, the provision of fair trials for all political prisoners,
the prevention of torture and the abolition of the death penalty.

Iran is a party to many international human rights instruments, among
them the ICCPR, the International Covenant on Economic, Social and Cultural
Rights, the Convention on the Prevention and Punishment of the Crime of
Genocide and the Geneva Conventions of 12 August 1949, and Relating to the
Protection of Victims of International Armed Conflicts. While these
covenants and treaties were signed or ratified before the Islamic Republic
came into being, their provisions are nevertheless binding on the present
government. The Islamic Republic of Iran has clearly demonstrated its
willingness to discuss compliance with these commitments by appearing in
1982 before the Human Rights Committee examining its compliance with the
provisions of the ICCPR, and more recently by allowing the visit of the UN
Special Representative.

It is of course impossible to argue against assertions, such as that
made by the Permanent Mission of the Islamic Republic of Iran to the UN in
New York in a letter to Amnesty International received on 9 August 1989,
that "there is no doubt that the divine faith of Islam, more than any other
man-made ideology, is responsive to human society in questions of legal
adjudication". It is not for Amnesty International to comment on matters
of religious faith, or to engage in comparisons of different ideologies or
systems. However, it is possible to observe that the way in which Islam is
applied to questions of legal adjudication differs widely between various
countries which claim Islamic Law as the basis of their legal systems, and
that there are different interpretations on how Islamic Law should be
applied within the Iranian Government itself.

For example, the punishment of amputation of the fingers has been
applied to dozens of convicted thieves in Iran in the past three years.
This punishment contravenes international human rights law because it has
been specifically identified by the Human Rights Committee as a form of
torture or cruel, inhuman or degrading punishment. One current of opinion
within Iran holds the view that the punishment of amputation is a deterrent
which it should not be necessary to use. Similarly, in an interview with

the Federal Republic of Germany's newspaper <u>Die Welt</u> on 10 August 1987, Hojatoleslam Rafsanjani is reported to have said that the punishment of stoning was imposed by "tasteless judges", and that this particularly cruel method of execution should not be used. Unfortunately, both these punishments continue to be applied in Iran, despite their incompatibility with international human rights standards being recognized by at least some government authorities. Very few other legal systems in the Islamic world apply these cruel, inhuman and degrading punishments. No other country is known by Amnesty International to have carried out a stoning to death since 1987. Saudi Arabia, Sudan and the Yemen Arab Republic are the only other countries which have carried out amputations as judicial punishments within the same period.

It is important not to overstate the extent of the problem posed by the supposed incompatibility of Islamic Law with international human rights standards. No interpretation of Islamic Law permits the imprisonment of innocent men and women, the torture or ill-treatment of prisoners (leaving aside judicial punishments which constitute torture or cruel, inhuman or degrading treatment), or the execution of people after unfair trials. There is a broad area of common understanding about what constitutes human rights abuse, and it is in this area that cooperation between the Iranian Government and the international human rights movement should take place, in the interest of upholding human rights standards. As the Iranian Government remarked to the Special Representative of the UN Human Rights Commission (as reported by the Special Representative in his report dated 26 January 1989):

> "Among the statements of the Iranian Government, the
> following deserves to be highlighted: 'matters raised
> by the Special Representative may still be considered in
> practical terms; there is no unsolvable complication
> stemming from the [in]compatibility between Islamic Law
> and international law." (UN document E/CN 4/1989/26,
> para 68)

The Iranian Government has not itself sought to avoid accountability for its human rights record by reference to Islam in many of the areas of primary concern to Amnesty International. Torture and arbitrary arrest are prohibited under the Constitution, and there are various constitutional guarantees designed to provide a fair trial for defendants. It is Amnesty International's contention that these constitutional safeguards have themselves been disregarded routinely, together with safeguards provided for by international human rights instruments, and that effective measures to ensure respect for these basic human rights principles should be implemented immediately.

5.2 Armed Opposition Groups and Human Rights

The activities of armed opposition groups are an emotive and difficult problem for any government. Armed attacks on government targets frequently result in the death or wounding of ordinary citizens, and it is not surprising that governments are often inclined to interpret any criticism of the tactics used by them to protect themselves and their citizens from the activities of armed opposition groups as being, at best, insensitive to the feelings of the victims of political violence or their relatives. At worst, such criticism of government policy may be seen as giving active support to a government's armed opponents. On the other hand, the need for international vigilance to seek to ensure that human rights standards are upheld even in the most demanding internal situations is clear, because it is in such situations of political instability that grave and wide-ranging human rights abuses most frequently occur.

Amnesty International has been challenged by many governments because it has spoken out against human rights violations suffered by supporters of armed opposition groups held in government custody while failing to condemn acts of political violence perpetrated by these groups. Governments have claimed that this approach is unbalanced.

Amnesty International has a consistent policy which it applies to all country situations with regard to human rights violations perpetrated by opposition groups. The organization condemns the torture or killing of prisoners by anyone. It brings its concerns with regard to such violations of human rights to the attention of those non-governmental entities which have assumed some of the characteristics of a government; such as control over a defined area of territory and the population within it, and the holding of prisoners.

The organization does not condone acts of violence carried out by opposition groups, such as murder in the pursuit of political objectives, and it recognizes that governments are responsible for bringing to justice those members of opposition groups who commit such criminal acts. However, the organization is concerned that this should be done in accordance with the law and with international human rights standards.

Amnesty International primarily seeks to ensure that governments respect their human rights commitments, partly because it is governments which are bound by the international human rights treaties on which the organization's work is based, but primarily because the organization is concerned about human rights violations suffered by individuals at the hands of the state. Governments consistently publicize violent acts by opposition groups and devote incomparably greater resources than Amnesty International's to that purpose, while individuals seeking redress for governmental abuses, often in the face of government evasion, have limited resources to draw upon.

The Iranian Government has responded to protests from Amnesty International about human rights abuses such as torture, arbitrary arrest or summary execution suffered by supporters of armed opposition groups, particularly the PMOI, by accusing the organization of "encouraging terrorism". For example the Permanent Mission of the Islamic Republic of Iran to the UN at New York wrote to Amnesty International in August 1989:

> "Providing protection and assistance to such groups...
> not only is not an effort towards preserving and promoting
> human rights but it clearly constitutes a flagrant violation
> of the rights of the victims of these groups... and
> encouragement of terrorism."

Amnesty International refutes the implication that by protesting about
human rights violations suffered by members and supporters of armed
opposition groups it is in any way supporting either the policies or the
methods of such groups. The organization is opposed to the torture or
execution of any prisoner regardless of the crime he or she may have
committed. The responsibility of the Iranian Government to respect the
human rights of all its citizens, including those guilty of criminal
activities on behalf of opposition groups, is not diminished by the actions
of armed opposition groups. On the contrary, Amnesty International
believes that in many countries there is a tendency for miscarriages of
justice to occur in criminal cases relating to the activities of political
opposition groups because of the intense pressure brought to bear on the
courts and the prosecution service to bring convictions for what may be
considered especially offensive crimes. This is one reason why Amnesty
International is particularly concerned that all political prisoners should
receive a fair and prompt trial.

The Deputy Minister for Foreign Affairs, Mohammad Hossein Lavassani,
was reported by the UN Special Representative in his interim report (UN
document A/44/620) to have asserted that the Iranian Government would not
answer allegations of human rights abuses if the source of these
allegations could be traced back to an armed opposition group:

> "Definitely the Islamic Republic of Iran cannot, and will not,
> hold itself committed to answering allegations originated from
> certain terrorist groups.
>
> "Allegations of human rights violations can be raised [only and]
> only after the terrorists have been excluded as the source...
> for the very holding of meetings with these groups and acquiring
> information is in effect a way of granting recognition to
> terrorism and sanctioning terrorism." (para 2)

The Special Representative found this approach unacceptable and so
does Amnesty International. The organization is concerned with human
rights violations suffered by individuals. It is committed to the
principle that whatever activities an individual may have been involved in
that person's fundamental human rights are not eroded. When Amnesty
International receives allegations of human rights violations of concern to
it then it investigates them, regardless of the source. The organization
is aware that it is in the interest of many opposition groups to spread
disinformation about governments. However, Amnesty International does not
simply repeat allegations made to it by any one source, rather it seeks to
substantiate or negate such allegations by reference to other sources, and
by comparing them with the body of information already in its files.

Amnesty International frequently seeks clarification from governments about allegations of human rights violations it has received. If the government refuses to answer Amnesty International's questions about specific allegations, as the Iranian Government has consistently done, then the organization inevitably must depend on sources which may not reflect the views of the government.

The Iranian Government has persistently failed to respond to requests by Amnesty International to be permitted to send a delegation to Iran to discuss its concerns about violations of human rights in Iran with responsible ministers and officials.

5.3   The Failure to Reply to Specific Inquiries

It is perhaps significant that the Iranian Government has replied to criticisms of its human rights record from Amnesty International and others only by putting forward general theoretical arguments about the inadmissibility of various types of criticism. What it has failed to do, and what Amnesty International regards as essential, is to respond to inquiries about specific human rights violations.

For example, in December 1988 Amnesty International submitted to the Iranian authorities a list of 325 prisoners reportedly executed during the mass killing of political prisoners after July 1988, seeking clarification of their fate. It has never received a reply from the authorities providing such information.

More recently, in August 1989 Amnesty International sought clarification from the Iranian authorities about allegations it had received that political prisoners had been executed ostensibly as drug-traffickers. As examples, it put forward the names of five men, giving the dates and places of execution. Amnesty International asked the Iranian authorities to be informed of the charges against the five and of the procedures followed at their trials. However, it received no reply. In the absence of any clarification from the Iranian Government about these cases, Amnesty International is as yet unable to form a conclusive opinion about the validity of allegations that political prisoners have been executed as drug-traffickers. Even requests for information about the beneficiaries of prisoner amnesties have remained unanswered.

Amnesty International has documented a consistent pattern of gross human rights violations in Iran over many years. Its information comes from a wide variety of sources including, extensively, reports in official Iranian newspapers and statements by Iranian Government officials. Amnesty International has no doubt that there is overwhelming evidence of continuing widespread human rights abuse in Iran and that, rather than simply asserting that respect for human rights is maintained in Iran, the government should take immediate steps to ensure full protection of the fundamental human rights of all its citizens.

CHAPTER SIX: SUMMARY OF RECOMMENDATIONS

More detailed recommendations are set out within the text and at the end of
relevant chapters. Many of the recommendations included in this report
were first published in Amnesty International's 1987 report on Iran: the
case for their implementation has been strengthened by a further three
years of human rights abuse.

6.1 The Death Penalty

Thousands of prisoners have been executed in Iran since 1987. In the six-
month period between July 1988 and January 1989 alone over 2,000 political
prisoners were executed in secret in all parts of the country. During 1989
over 1,500 criminal executions were officially announced, more than 1,000
of them for drug-trafficking offences. Large numbers of executions
continue to take place.

   Many prisoners have been executed after trials which failed to satisfy
minimum international standards for fair trial.

-    Amnesty International is opposed to the death penalty in all
     circumstances, regarding it as the ultimate form of cruel, inhuman or
     degrading punishment. Its primary recommendation in this area is that
     the Government of the Islamic Republic of Iran should demonstrate its
     respect for the inherent right to life by putting an immediate end to
     executions.

-    Pending the implementation of such a decision, Amnesty International
     recommends that all trials in capital cases should respect, as a
     minimum standard, the provisions of Articles 6, 14, and 15 of the
     ICCPR, so as to guarantee the safeguards afforded by a fair trial for
     those accused in capital cases, including the right to seek pardon or
     commutation of the death sentence, and to the conviction being
     reviewed by a higher tribunal.

Amnesty International opposes unreservedly the extrajudicial killing of any
individual on political grounds by governments. Since 1987 a number of
Iranian opposition personalities in exile have been attacked, and in some
cases killed, apparently by agents of the Iranian Government.

-    Amnesty International urges the Iranian authorities to condemn
     publicly the practice of extrajudicial executions, and to make clear
     to all government officials in Iran and abroad that such killings will
     not be tolerated.

6.2 Unfair Trials

The failure of the Iranian judicial system to provide adequate safeguards
for defendants facing trial in capital cases, and in trials of political
prisoners, is one of the fundamental reasons for the prevalence of wide-
ranging human rights abuses in Iran.

Amnesty International is disturbed by the numerous and consistent reports of summary trials of political prisoners, particularly those taking place before Islamic Revolutionary Courts. It considers that the Administrative Regulations Governing Revolutionary Courts and the Public Prosecutor's Offices contain inadequate provisions to ensure fair trials, and even the basic safeguards established by law are not applied.

- Amnesty International recommends that all exceptional courts, including Islamic Revolutionary Courts, should be abolished so as to consolidate judicial proceedings into one system, within the law, which should provide all the safeguards necessary for fair trial.

6.3 Political Imprisonment

Many political arrests take place in secret making it difficult to quantify the number of political prisoners in Iran. Countless victims of arbitrary arrest, including many prisoners of conscience, remain in prison years after their arrest. Some have been sentenced to long prison terms after unfair trials by revolutionary courts; some are simply held indefinitely without charge or trial, or long after their sentences have expired.

Political arrests are carried out in an arbitrary manner by the Islamic Revolutionary Committees and by the IRGC. Freedom of political activity has been circumscribed by the widespread imprisonment of prisoners of conscience.

- Amnesty International recommends that effective measures should be taken to put an end to arbitary arrest: for example, respect for Article 32 of the Constitution of the Islamic Republic of Iran which requires that any arrest be approved by a judicial authority, and that reasons for the arrest must be communicated in writing to the prisoner and elucidated to him.

- Amnesty International urges that all prisoners of conscience should be released immediately and unconditionally. The organization recommends that the continuing detention of all political prisoners should be reviewed by an independent judicial authority empowered to order the immediate release of those against whom there is no evidence of their having committed any recognizably criminal offence.   In other cases, where such a review concludes that there is a case to be answered by the prisoner, a fair trial in accordance with international standards should be held.

6.4 Torture

Torture, beating and intimidation of prisoners is reportedly widespread both during pre-trial detention and following trial and judgment. There is a wide range of measures which should be taken to minimize the risk of torture occuring.

-   Amnesty International recommends that incommunicado detention should
    be strictly controlled; all prisoners should be granted prompt and
    regular access to legal counsel of their own choosing and to
    relatives.

-   A public and impartial investigation should be conducted into
    allegations of torture. Its results should be made public, and any
    members of the security or other forces implicated as being involved
    in torture should be brought to justice.

-   Prisons and detention centres should be regularly inspected by an
    independent authority empowered to seek redress for prisoners'
    complaints.

-   The Government of the Islamic Republic of Iran should become a party
    to the UN Convention against Torture and comply with its provisions,
    and should further be guided by the recommendations of the UN Special
    Rapporteur on torture, particularly those contained in his 18 December
    1989 report (see Chapter 4).

Amputation and flogging are forms of torture or cruel, inhuman or degrading
punishment prohibited by international law.

-   Amnesty International recommends the replacement of such punishments
    by other penalties which are consistent with recognized international
    standards for the prevention and punishment of crime and the treatment
    of offenders.

APPENDIX: <u>ABBREVIATIONS USED IN TEXT</u>

ADFSIN	Association for the Defence of Freedom and Sovereignty of the Iranian Nation
ECOSOC	UN Economic and Social Council
ICCPR	International Covenant on Civil and Political Rights
IRCG	Islamic Revolutionary Guards Corps
KDPI	Kurdish Democratic Party of Iran
PFOI	People's Fedaiyan Organization of Iran
PMOI	People's Mojahedine Organisation of Iran
UN	United Nations

Information from Amnesty International

This paper is part of Amnesty International's publications program. As part of its effort to mobilize world public opinion in defence of the victims of human rights violations, Amnesty International produces a monthly Newsletter, an annual report, and reports, briefings and other documents on countries in all quarters of the globe.

Amnesty International attaches great importance to impartial and accurate reporting of facts. Its activities depend on meticulous research into allegations of human rights violations. The International Secretariat in London (with a staff of over 250, comprising some 40 nationalities) has a Research Department which collects and analyses information from a wide variety of sources. These include hundreds of newspapers and journals, government bulletins, transcriptions of radio broadcasts, reports from lawyers and humanitarian organizations, as well as letters from prisoners and their families. Amnesty International also visits countries to carry out research, observe trials, meet prisoners and interview government officials. Amnesty International takes full responsibility for its published reports and if proved wrong on any point is prepared to issue a correction.

How to subscribe to Amnesty International

A subscription to Amnesty International will give you access to information about human rights abuses produced on a global, independent and impartial basis. You will also receive details on how you can help the people who are the victims.

Amnesty International Newsletter

This monthly bulletin is a regular update on Amnesty International's work: reports of fact-finding visits, details of political prisoners, reliable reports of torture and executions. It is written — without political bias — for human rights activists throughout the world and is widely used by journalists, students, political leaders, doctors, lawyers and other professionals.

Amnesty International Report

This annual report is a country-by-country survey of Amnesty International's work to combat political imprisonment, torture and the death penalty throughout the world. In describing the organization's work, the report provides details of human rights abuses in over 130 countries. It is probably the most widely read — and most influential — of the many reports published by Amnesty International each year.

Please detach this form and return to the Amnesty International section in your country or to: Amnesty International Publications, 1 Easton Street, London WC1X 8DJ, United Kingdom.

☐ I wish to subscribe to the *Amnesty International Newsletter* (price, including postage and packing: £7.00, US $12.00).
☐ I wish to subscribe to the monthly *Amnesty International Newsletter* and yearly *Amnesty International Report* (price, including postage and packing: £18.00, US$30.00).
☐ Please send me further details of Amnesty International Publications.

Name —————————————————————— **Address** ——————————————————————

——————————————————————————————————————

——————————————————————————————————————